FOR MUSICIANS ONLY

FOR MUSICIANS ONLY

Claudia Suzanne, Thomas Stein, and Michael Niehaus

BILLBOARD PUBLICATIONS, INC./NEW YORK

About the Authors

Claudia Suzanne is an instrumentalist, singer, lyricist, and production coordinator who heads a California-based music management and production company.

Michael Niehaus is a sound engineer, stage and road manager, and music consultant. His credits include the Eagles, Ricky Nelson, Elvin Bishop, and the heavy metal bands Ratt and Motley Crue.

Thomas Stein is a pianist, vocalist, composer, and sound technician currently featured in a successful and long-running act in Southern California.

Copyright © 1988 by Claudia S. Stein, Thomas A. Stein, and Michael N. Niehaus.

First published 1988 by Billboard Publications, Inc., 1515 Broadway, New York, New York 10036.

Library of Congress Cataloging-in-Publication Data

Suzanne, Claudia.
  For musicians only / Claudia Suzanne, Thomas A. Stein, Michael N. Niehaus.
    p. cm.
  Bibliography: p.
  Includes index.
  ISBN 0-8230-7548-6 (pbk.)
  1. Popular music—Vocational guidance. I. Stein, Thomas A. II. Niehaus, Michael N. III. Title.
ML3795.S9 1986
780'.42'023—dc19

Manufactured in the United States of America

First printing, 1988

1 2 3 4 5 6 7 8 9/93 92 91 90 89 88

To our parents
and Bear (who got us
over the border twice)

.

Table of Contents

Foreword

THE PROBLEM with the music business is that everyone knows something about it and no one knows everything about it. There is no place that you can go for all the answers because there are too many right answers for every question . . . and even more wrong ones. Schools teach plenty about music theory, notation, and instrumental technique, but they teach very little about the music business. Unlike most other fields of endeavor, the music business rarely provides a "company" situation in which you can move up slowly as you learn. It is even more unusual to find an established, older musician who will take you under his or her wing and show you the ropes. No matter what your contract says, being in music means being self-employed. The only absolute rule is: all gigs end.

The most common road to knowledge in this business is the one built on trial and error. Trial and error is incredibly time-consuming, and is the main reason music is such a transient field. Music is also the field of the young: you play in a band or "gig around" for a few years until you've had enough and finally settle down to something considered to be more serious. Having a band is a great way to work your way through college. Unfortunately, many musicians stop playing after college and never pick up their axes again except at occasional parties. Nevertheless, you can have a serious career in music, even without being a star, if you approach it as just that—a career.

Toward that end, this book is written for those instrumentalists and vocalists who want to make a living playing music, who are looking for starting points to their careers, and are in need of the basic commercial tools of the trade. It is written by musicians who wish they had had a similar book at the beginning of their own careers.

The book necessarily generalizes. For any given situation, dozens of effective responses or solutions can apply. Therefore, it is assumed that as a serious musician you are willing to put in the time and mental effort necessary to weigh your own situation against the examples given in the book.

It is understood that you've probably achieved proficiency on your axe, know what kind of music you play best, know how to develop your chops, and are ready for the next step. It is also assumed that you've read or heard enough to know the meaning of music industry "buzz" words used in the text (such as axe, chops, and gig).

This book is primarily for musicians and vocalists in the rock, country, rhythm and blues, pop, and related fields. Classical, gospel, and jazz musicians have other paths to follow, although they will probably find some of the information here familiar and helpful.

For purposes of brevity, the term "musician" includes vocalists. The pronoun "he" is used to indicate either sex as it applies to the reader. The words "group" or "band" refer to any organization of musicians, singers, or combination thereof that is complete within itself for purposes of performance—not necessarily recording.

1

THE
BUSINESS

Wouldn't it be wonderful if musical talent were all you needed for a successful career? Even the most naive beginner knows it doesn't work that way. As much as you need musical proficiency, you need insight into the world of business. You have to have the skill to build and run a band; an awareness of politics and the power of leverage; a realistic and challenging career plan; and the ability to work with people and to gear yourself to a variety of professional situations, from clubs to recording studios. A life in music requires much more than creative and technical skill. As John Candy once said, "It's not show art. It's show business."

Running a Band

THE MUSIC BUSINESS is based on people. Choosing the right people to work with who have the right abilities and attitudes is probably the most important decision you'll make in your musical career, and you may have to make it dozens of times. A musical unit is made up not of instruments, but of the people who play them, and each individual has different needs, goals, and methods of working. Building and running a successful unit, which is only the first step in a very long process toward success in the business, can monopolize all your time and energy. You, as an individual, must find the way to be part of the you, as a group, which will work together effectively and productively. Even a solo vocalist has to have a reliable accompanist or backup group that he can depend on to function correctly and effectively.

FORMING A BAND

There are four basic models for forming a band: a group composed of friends; the leader and sidemen formula; the "corporate rock" idea; the coordination of a partnership (a marriage of convenience).

A Group of Friends. Groups composed of friends have a tendency to be "first band" groups. Except in rare cases, they have poor track records for staying together all the way to the top. However, this kind of group can be an important training ground for honing your instrumental, vocal, political, stage, and business skills.

To be successful there are several rules to follow. Make sure that all group members are willing to play the same music. Don't try to make one member compromise his preferences, and don't attempt to accommodate everyone's esoteric tastes. Don't try to swing the repertoire, for example, all the way from the bass player's love of jazz to the keyboard player's love of heavy metal. There should be one basic theme in mind. Make sure you can be categorized by any audience. Usually, a natural leader will emerge, but if this doesn't happen, appoint a leader by popular vote. One person should represent the band in such business (gig) situations as signing the contracts and collecting the money.

▶ *Positives:* Since you are all friends or acquaintances, no one has to get used to strangers. You know each other and can easily develop a "family" feeling within the band. Since you already like each other, the personal warmth of your friendship can spill over into your music, making even a tepid performance come off as okay. You have a built-in emotional support system as well as a broader friend-and-family base for an initial audience or following. Of course, another major advantage is that everyone should be easy to reach and gather together for rehearsals.

▶ *Negatives:* Being in a band together can kill a friendship—even several. Friends are not always on the same level of talent or ability; they don't all necessarily develop at the same rate. Your band will quickly become stagnant without new ideas and input from outside the clique. Personal problems, such as girlfriend and boyfriend squabbles, can interfere with or destroy your professional relationships. It is very difficult to fire a friend and keep the friendship. It is very difficult to fire a friend, period. Another negative that you might not consider until it's too late is the difficulty of progressing from the "party" stage of jamming with your friends to the professional performance level, where your career can be taken seriously.

Leader and Sidemen. The best-known band formula is undoubtedly that of leader and sidemen. Any musician or vocalist who wants to do the bulk of the work, take the bulk of the responsibilities, and garner the bulk of the spotlight or credit can put together a leader and sidemen group. The leader is usually the person with the leverage or the gig, the person who owns or controls the band name. Theoretically, the leader hires the people in the group, determines the platform and instrumentation, gets the gigs, pays the money, decides which tunes go in and which don't, and fires those people who cause problems or don't measure up. The leader may or may not involve the other band members in the decisions that go down. It is also important to remember that the leader will pay the sidemen according to individual agreements, not according to a split in the take. So a bass player who gets fifty dollars a night has no basis for complaint when he finds out the drummer is making sixty dollars; the bass player and drummer made separate agreements with the person who hired them—the leader.

▶ *Positives:* If you have a good leader, you can have a successful band. From the leader's point of view, this kind of group offers continuity. He can replace and handpick his sidemen and choose a format to best show off the band's talents. If one player—even an important one— leaves the group, the leader still controls the core and can hire a replacement of his choosing. Of course, this implies a great deal of responsibility: if he doesn't replace the player and keep the group working, he might lose everyone through attrition. The leader can solve this kind of problem ahead of time by keeping the number of sidemen down to a predetermined level of importance through duplication of abilities within the group. Then when someone leaves, that person's part can be temporarily handled by a remaining band member. The leader can then replace the missing player as soon as possible.

From the sideman's point of view, the advantages of a leader and sidemen group aren't bad either. He doesn't have to handle any business or look for work. He has flexibility and the freedom of group-to-group movement. He doesn't have to worry about friendship and loyalty factors or format changes. If the group is out of work for too long or he doesn't like the way the guitarist plays, he can move on without undue emotional or professional problems.

▶ *Negatives:* A group is only as good as its leader. If the leader doesn't cut it on a performance, personal, or business level; if he can't keep the group working; if he hires the wrong people or the right people for the wrong reasons; if he picks the wrong tunes or has the wrong people sing them; then the group isn't going to be a success even at the beginning stage. If you are the leader, you are responsible for everything. You will be blamed for everything. You will be bad-mouthed the most and your reputation will be on the line constantly.

If you are the sideman the disadvantages for you are simpler and more specific. You have little artistic control and no business control, period.

Corporate Rock. The corporate rock idea works like this: a financier owns and, perhaps, organizes the group. The financier owns all the major equipment. He picks the musicians, promotes the band, finds the material, and, theoretically, catapults the band to stardom, if only briefly or locally. To be picked for such a group you must be politically and professionally adept, be the right age, have the right look, and present the right attitude.

▶ *Positives:* This is probably a moneymaking venture. You have joined an elite group that has all the elements necessary to advance from being a band to being a hit (if faceless) group. You have no worries about business matters, except to follow directions. You will undoubtedly get the opportunity to make a great deal of money, which, if handled correctly, can be invested for slower times. Being part of a corporate rock situation can be an impetus for future career moves to more self-directed situations.

▶ *Negatives:* You have little artistic and no business control except by contracted agreement (for example, you've been signed to write or arrange the tunes). Your success or failure is dependent on the controlling person's abilities, contracts, and financial status. You have tenuous job security since most faceless bands change members without the public knowing it, at least before they hit it big. You have to keep in mind that you are part not of an artistic product, but of a commercial product developed to fill a specific need. The longevity of a corporate rock band depends on the ebb and flow of popular tastes, not on the abilities, ingenuity, or performance of the individual musician.

Coordination of a Partnership. The coordination of a partnership (a marriage of convenience) is very common in the clubs today. This arrangement is more a matter of the room hiring musicians than the musicians putting something together ahead of time. Musicians and singers get together for a specific gig or audition. There is no actual leader other than the person who has the contact for the gig. The money gets split equally. The instrumentation and musical format are determined by the needs of the gig. The repertoire usually starts out being mutually known tunes and a few new tunes learned for the audition or the first week of work, then develops as the room dictates. Eventually, a tacit understanding of leadership will arise.

▶ *Positives:* You can have a lot of artistic control simply by taking that control within the structure that the room dictates. You can also keep things very professional and nonpersonal, thereby developing leverage for your own career. Because of the compromise situation that you're in, you can all satisfy your musical needs to a point, even if they are diverse. And if things look like they're not going to work out or the gig is drying up, you can drop out of this group and move into another one with no qualms.

▶ *Negatives:* There is no strong force holding this group together beyond the specific gig, so it is really a short-term situation even if you become a house band. There is no long-term mutual goal, and that translates into lessened input for the current project, or a state of professional limbo. Since the unit was put together only for this gig you have little control over the other members of the group unless you happened to have landed the gig.

There is always the chance that the group will click and continue as a group to other rooms and bigger and better things. For that to happen, however, a leader must emerge to search for work, create promotion, and handle the business end. Equally divided money, expenses, chores, and spotlights are terrific in theory, but can lead to nonproductivity and inertia.

You should only go into this kind of partnership if you are sure you can get along with your partners. A marriage of convenience is a good breeding ground for personnel problems because there is a power vacuum. There is also a definite job security problem since no one need make a commitment to stay with the gig if something better comes along. In order for this kind of group to persevere, it must evolve into a new form—one that involves a leader.

PERSONNEL PROBLEMS

Whatever type of group you are in may eventually transform into a successful self-run band, that is, a group of musicians who have finally found the right combination of instrumentation and personnel; the natural business leader; the natural "star"; and the natural backup people who are all into the same music, the same goals, and the same methods of reaching them. At that point you can proceed toward developing your band's career. Many musicians never reach that point. You can make it your business to reach that point. The biggest stumbling blocks you will have will be personnel problems.

There are many types of problems that arise when working with humans, especially when those humans are in a business based on showing off their own talents. The most common and hardest to correct are attitude problems. Lack of enthusiasm, egotism, snobbery, and burnout are all aspects of unprofessional behavior with which every musician has to contend at one point or another. Coping effectively with the attitude problems of band members is difficult and can be frustrating. And of course, there is the obvious problem of drugs. Can a musician be successful using drugs? How will they affect career advancement?

Negative Attitudes. Tardiness, lack of enthusiasm or commitment, and laziness can translate into anything from being late for rehearsal to not showing up for the gig. A player may not get his part down in time for a performance or may be so lackadaisical toward new material or "putting out" on stage that he dampens everyone else's spirits and creates anger and frustration.

If you have a group comprised of friends, the best thing you can do is to get the entire group to have a heart-to-heart talk with the culprit. Do not send a designated representative. Designated representatives run many risks in friendship groups. You should never volunteer to be one. If you designate a representative you can't be sure what that person will really say or how forcefully the point will really come down. Nor can you know to what extent the other members will back up the representative when push comes to shove. Economic sanctions, such as fines for being late or partial loss of pay for not knowing material, may have some influence in the short term, but probably won't change the member's attitude in a positive way over the long haul. If the heart-to-heart talk doesn't produce results, then a group meeting should be held to decide if that person is going to remain a part of the group. If you do decide to keep someone who is always late or who lacks enthusiasm, be aware that you've made a decision to limit the future success of your entire group.

If you're in a leader and sidemen situation and it's the leader who is late or unenthusiastic, you have two choices: leave the group or tolerate the situation. If the group is successful, then you might just want to wait it out until something better comes along. Start looking for that something better immediately and discreetly, however, because your leader's attitude is a sign of unprofessionalism, which will restrict the group's advancement. If it is one of the sidemen who has the attitude problem and you are the leader, talk to him. Remember to pick the time, place, and phrasing carefully so that you are effective without creating anger or putting your own or the group's position in jeopardy. Make this a private conversation. Judging from his reaction to your initial discussion, either give him a chance to correct his behavior or immediately start to discreetly look for a replacement without letting any—and that means any—of the other members know. If you are a sideman working with another sideman who has attitude problems and your leader doesn't know how to handle it, you're in a no-win situation. Get out or be tolerant, whichever is most feasible for your own interests.

In a corporate rock situation, life is easy. You can report the problem member, then forget it. You are not in a position to do anything about it. This is one of the advantages, and disadvantages, of corporate rock. On the other hand, be careful about whom you are reporting, and to whom. Your own job could be in jeopardy as a result of reporting someone else's bad habits. Watch the politics of the situation and know who is favored and who is not. Are you?

When you're working in a coordination of partners, the lazy habits of a partner can present a difficult situation. You can't fire someone you didn't hire. The question is whether or not the job is in jeopardy. If it is, and you're sure replacing that partner will secure the gig, then you as a group can decide to replace him before the job is lost. If the gig is not in jeopardy, then the person is probably doing exactly what the room wants with his laid-back attitude, whether you like it or not. In a marriage of convenience, you don't have much leverage for changing what works on the gig. If the group is about to lose the gig and you are not satisfied with one or more of the partners, you will simply go on to a new group anyway. Again, this is one of the disadvantages of this type of band.

The Prima Donna. Other personnel problems revolve around the "prima donna" personality, along with attitudes of snobbery, egotism, and a tendency toward one-upmanship. First, bear in mind that a true "star" must have a bit of all these traits. Talent must balance out ego and vice versa. On the other hand, if your prima donna is the percussionist, or a bass player who doesn't sing, or a player or singer who is just not that terrific, you've got a problem.

Let's be real. Once an individual has become a snob or a prima donna, the situation is irreversible. People do not usually become humble while onstage, certainly not on demand. If someone has started to play one-upmanship, he's probably not going to stop. So the initial questions must be: Is this person a major contributing factor to the group's success? Is he holding the group back? Or is he just holding on? In other words, is all that ego helping or not? If it is, then you have to accept the fact that you're working with a "star," however small. If it's not, then you're working with someone who is trying to bully or bluff his way along and you're faced with an attitude problem to be handled.

If you're in a friend group your friendship is about to be strained, whether you speak up or not. In fact, in any kind of unit—friends, leader and sidemen, corporate rock, or marriage of convenience—a snob who is not the star of the show and who is not advancing your product is a hindrance to be excised. If he is your friend, you'll have to find a way to resolve your professional relationship before you lose that and the friendship. This kind of problem is an excellent example of why friend groups dissolve.

If you're in a leader and sidemen situation and you're the leader, you've made a hiring mistake. Discreetly find a replacement. The sidemen will have to make their own decisions regarding the length of time they're willing to tolerate the problem before leaving.

In a coordination of partners, your hands are tied unless you want to quit the gig. This kind of group can be absolute heaven if the right combination gets together to create a happy, longstanding house band. If not, it can be real hell on wheels to deal with all the personnel problems.

If you're in a corporate rock band, again this problem will be handled by the powers-that-be. The best thing about working with someone who thinks he's God's gift to the music world is that if he isn't, he can't hold up the facade very long.

Burnout. Burnout is having used up your enthusiasm for what you're doing, at least for the time being. It's a good indication that a particular phase of your career is over, regardless of what that career is. You will have to reinvent the situation or come back to the old one with a new focus.

If you try to force a player who is burned out to continue on the same path, you will find that you're engaging in an exercise in futility. This is true no matter what kind of band you are in. The person who is burned out is probably expecting to—maybe even hoping to—leave the band, or at least the phase it's in. Take a good look at where you are as a group. Are you going somewhere with your career or just holding on to the same position? Or are you actually losing ground? If the bass player is burned out, is it because he's tired of working clubs, tired of the repertoire, tired of the management of the band, tired of the whole group, or tired of being a bass player?

Burnout is a touchy and personal problem that is normally handled by the individual who is affected, rather than by the rest of the group. The usual response is to quit either the band or the business. What should you do if you feel burned out? Try a new group. Try a new type of music—country instead of R&B, heavy metal instead of pop-rock. Try a new area with a different type of club. Take some time off and learn about some of the things that nonmusicians do such as eating, sleeping, and going to movies at night. If you find you simply must play again, then you were burned out not on the business but on your former circumstances. If, however, you find that you can live without the long hours, the low pay, the lack of appreciation, and the heartaches (not to mention the glamour), then by all means leave the performance arena and let yourself have a normal, happy life. Lots of people do it; it's no disgrace. Most of the people who enter the music business will not succeed. If you get too worn out to care if you make it or not, try going for personal happiness instead and look back on a valiant and enjoyable effort. If, however, there is something inside you that won't let you rest unless you're on stage, then take a totally different tack when you go back. "Weekend warriors" work day jobs all week, play on the weekends, and can eat and have their music, too. Switching from heavy metal in dance rooms to middle-of-the-road

(MOR) in intimate lounges may be the key. The point to remember is that if you've burned out once, returning to your old stomping grounds is not likely to satisfy you for very long.

Drugs and Alcohol. Here we have a problem that most musicians will encounter at some point in their careers: the pervasive use of drugs and alcohol in the music business. Involvement with these substances can have serious consequences from the standpoint of the law, your performing ability, getting along with other musicians, and overall career advancement.

From a legal point of view, if you use drugs you are open to danger on the way to the job, at the job, on the stage, and on the way home from the job. Getting drunk on stage and driving home is an obvious way to trash a career and a life under any circumstances, and in these days of police vigilance it is especially risky. Undercover cops have no problem blending into an audience and watching a drug deal go down out back, or winding up in the john during a break when you're trying to snort a line. You can get busted. The club can get busted. The other musicians who don't even use drugs can get busted. When you're busted in a musical situation, your equipment can be impounded. If you're busted on stage (it happens) the whole band can be arrested. And guess what? The owner probably won't hold the gig for you.

On higher career levels, the risks may be more pronounced. Not only are you endangering your hard-earned reputation, but you may also be liable for the substantial cost of returned tickets if you miss a scheduled concert performance.

Then there are the consequences of being arrested. We have all seen enough movies to know that you run the risk of injury if you have to spend time in jail—injury that could negate your career. It takes very little to disable a musician: a broken hand or a few broken fingers can finish a keyboard player. Jail time does happen, and you already have one strike against you in a court of law because you are a musician.

Never forget that society at large still views musicians as people who play instead of work. The overall image to the public is not in your favor.

Getting caught is probably not one of your big worries because you know how to be discreet, right? And some people claim that a couple of hits or a line or two makes you play better, push longer, and enjoy the music more. The fact is, from a musical point of view, mind-altering substances give you a false perception of your actual performance. You may think that you're playing on a much higher level than you do without drugs. The problem is that reliance on drugs diminishes your control, so that there is no way to recapture the performance that you thought was so wonderful. The next time you do the drug, you may not get the same results. Then again, you may indeed play the same way, which could be disastrous if you were unaware that you were playing poorly.

Major problems on stage from using drugs include: erratic mood shifts (the guitar player who suddenly gets furious because he doesn't sing the next tune), memory loss (forgetting where the bridge comes in or how to come back out of the solo), loss of dexterity ("Boy, is she missing notes tonight!"), paranoia ("I think someone's fooled with the equipment"; "Maybe they're just auditioning us"; "My God, we're going to get notice!"), and loss of professional control and an objective perception of what you're really doing. These all add up to what may be a brilliant performance from your point of view and an embarrassing, innocuous, or simply uninspired performance as far as the audience or club owner is concerned.

Some people believe that there are physical benefits from certain substances when used in moderation. But when you're talking about a musical career and your drugs have become more important to you than your axe or the music, you are way beyond moderation: the dope is a distracting element on stage or off the stage. It is a fact that the high you get from cocaine, for example, will be in direct proportion to the low that will result coming down. So a high on stage can result in your being nonfunctional during critical rehearsal or business time. This can be compensated for, of course, by more drugs, but now we're getting into serious drug problems.

What it boils down to is this: if you are using drugs to the point where your perception is out of whack, your performance is impaired, your offstage time is unreliable, or you feel the stage is melting under your feet, then you have a major problem. In addition, you are a problem, and at the very least you can expect to have difficulty advancing beyond where you are now, even if you do manage to maintain your current status. At the extreme, you have no place in front of an audience, and only a lot of support money will keep you there for long. Ergo, you've trashed your career.

You are probably saying to yourself that this is all propaganda, that you've heard this gloom-and-doom stuff before and that it doesn't apply to you. If it truly doesn't apply, then you're in good shape, because from a political point of view, people will stop working with you if you are a hazard to their careers and to their lives. On the other hand, people may shun you if you are a belligerent nonuser; moral "crusaders" make musicians uncomfortable. You must find a path that combines personal control with whatever tolerance of others is necessary for political purposes. This doesn't mean acceptance of dangerous behavior or circumstances, nor does it mean that your peers will be as controlled or as tolerant.

If one of the other members of your band is functioning poorly due to drug or alcohol use, then your group has to decide how and when to replace him. As with attitude problems, the way you deal with this situation will depend on the type of group you're in. But whatever the structure of your group, if you decide to keep working with someone who cannot control his own abilities and behavior, you have obviously made another decision that will negate success.

One final word on the subject of drugs and career advancement: it is certainly to someone else's advantage to have you under the influence when talking business. This is true even if he is under the influence himself, or has led you to believe that he is. You have relinquished control over the proceedings, and the psychological advantage is all his. This gives him leverage; leverage controls the business world; music is a business. A person who allows himself to be lulled by three martinis or paid off partly in money, partly in cocaine, is not just a fool, he has abdicated his career.

THE LEADER'S RESPONSIBILITIES

The tasks of the leader may involve minor inconveniences as well as major undertakings. Such responsibilities include selecting a musical platform; hiring and firing musicians; handling the money and subsequent tax reporting; and being aware of insurance needs and club liability in the event of fire, theft, or vandalism.

Selecting a Platform. You know what kind of music you like to play, and you probably (hopefully) know what you play the best. Unfortunately, what you like may not be what is selling right now, and you find yourself out there every night playing music for which you have little feeling. This is hard on the intestines. Unhappily, it is a common situation. When you are starting a band with the purpose of making money in the clubs, your platform, or musical focus, will be dictated by the radio: whatever is on the local top 40 station is in your repertoire. If, however, you are starting a band to play the music you love and perform the best, you have much more freedom with your repertoire . . . probably too much. Many groups make the mistake of being undefinable. It is hard to advance in the business if someone can't pinpoint where you're coming from.

As the leader of a group, it is your responsibility to develop and maintain the group's platform through all repertoire changes. This means centering in on a type or style of music, such as country, rock, R&B, pop, or ethnic, and then finding a groove within that style. If you're inclined toward country, for example, you can play country pop, country rock, country and western, bluegrass, down-home twang, American roots music, or folk. If you're into rock, you can pick from a range of styles that includes heavy metal, punk, acid, pop, rock 'n' roll, and oldies but moldies. Rhythm and blues styles range from almost jazz to almost gospel, pop, fusion, and blues. Pop music also has a number of different classifications, among them are bubble gum, ballads, techno-pop, and new wave. There are literally dozens of ethnic styles, including reggae, Latin, salsa, Italian, and Greek.

If you find the groove that you easily fit into, you will have less trouble defining and communicating with your audience. You'll have less trouble deciding which songs to put into your repertoire and what songs to pass on. Of course, if you're playing five hours a night, five nights a week in a neighborhood club or for a corporate chain that hands you a required song list, you'll have to have more flexibility than when you're showcasing your group in the interest of career advancement. That's just the way the gig goes. It's important to remember two things. The first is that when you've picked your groove, hire people who are into that same groove. Don't hire someone who is great on his axe but loves an entirely different style of music than you do. You're asking for personnel problems from the beginning. Second, if your roots are in jazz, gospel, classical, opera, or any other type of relatively noncommercial music, try to avoid letting that love destroy the music you have to play to make a living. All music has validity for the musicians who love it and for the audience who appreciates it. Enjoy what you have to do as much as you can and learn whatever you can from it. Any performance or musical knowledge you acquire can only enhance your ability to perform the music you really love.

Auditioning and Hiring Musicians. There are many reasons why you may need to acquire a new musician or two. You could be starting a band from scratch. You might have need for an emergency replacement because of illness or death or a strange disappearance. You may want to replace someone because of extended personnel problems or for political reasons. The group might want to change or redefine its style or perhaps just expand to accommodate new musical forms. In any event, there are as many ways of finding musicians as there are reasons for needing them. You can advertise in trade magazines, use a local contact service, call the musicians' union, check with nearby colleges, appropriate from other bands, or spread the need by word-of-mouth. Sooner or later, though, you're going to have to audition musicians.

When you need to acquire personnel, for whatever reason, remember that time is always of the essence if you want to maintain momentum. Each band or musical project has its own life and death. It is a fact that if a group doesn't come together quickly, nothing else will happen quickly.

When you're ready, stage an open audition, or cattle call. Cattle calls are the norm of the industry, and they are an exasperating, frustrating experience for the auditionee, but an incredibly useful tool for the auditioner. First of all, a cattle call expedites the hiring process and allows you to pick and choose more freely. Additionally, staging a cattle call is a definite display of power, which is something you want to project initially. There is always time to get friendly after you've hired the person you're going to get friendly with. The odds are good that you will find the right person through back-to-back assembly-line auditioning, and it will be just as easy as if you'd taken a longer period of time. If you stage the cattle call correctly, all the benefits are on your side.

Book the appointments an hour apart and give them each forty-five minutes. You don't have to use the entire forty-five minutes for everyone; give yourself a break when you need it. Take notes on everyone who auditions. Don't stop the auditioning just because you think you found the right person on the second or third try. Don't make special allowances for anyone; that is, don't let the person auditioning get the upper hand, psychologically. If, for example, one of the candidates blows you away with his musicianship, don't let his incredible talent influence you to hire him on the spot. He may be wrong for your group in other ways. Never commit to anything at the audition and don't say that you'll call back either way. You're not going to call back if they didn't get the job. Tell them you'll call if they've got the gig. Reaudition all final candidates, if possible.

Auditioning is usually a crisis situation. In fact, auditioning should be a crisis situation for the person being considered. Crisis plus observation equals truth. If a person can't handle the audition, chances are that sometime onstage when the chips are down, he won't be able to take the pressure.

If at all possible, have the person you select meet with the other members of the band to make sure they all get along. This is necessary regardless of how good a player the new guy is. People make music; technical ability doesn't. Bringing in the wrong personality will only lead you quickly to another audition situation.

Face it. You're going to make errors in hiring. While a crisis situation may be a good tool for determining ability under pressure, it isn't the same as daily performance or weekly rehearsal pressure. Always hire a new member on probation: "We'll see how it works out" or "Let's give it a try for awhile." Don't relinquish your power base; it's not to your advantage to extend long-term commitments based on short-term evaluations.

As you go through these auditions and make your notes, pay attention to the following:

▶ *Looks:* Does the person fit with the rest of the band?

▶ *Ability:* Can he pull off the music you play? Can he learn it easily, using the method you normally use? Is his technique so far beyond your needs that he's going to be bored quickly?

▶ *Musical Compatibility:* Does he like the stuff you play? Is it what he's been playing or just what he's willing to play at the moment?

▶ *Attitudes:* How does he feel about the kind of gigs you're currently doing and the kind you're aiming for? What is his feeling about you as a leader? What is his attitude? How does he feel about rehearsals, adding new songs, changing things around, and getting to the gig on time? Is his work ethic compatible with yours? This especially can be a hurdle if you play five nights a week and he works a full-time day gig, or if you want to push for career advancement through selected, infrequent gigs and he needs to make his living playing music.

Make enough notes on each person to be able to remember who they are at the end of the audition surge. Of course if you're in an emergency situation you won't have time for all of this.

It is the responsibility of the leader of a group to always have a contingency plan for the loss of any musician. In order to replace someone in an emergency or in due course, you will have to have on hand some accurate representation of the band's performance. This translates into live tapes of all your tunes and as many charts as possible. A video of the band working live—to use not as a sales tool, but as a learning tool—will give the new player a fast way of blending in with the group.

Always have someone ready to do an emergency replacement, even if he's not the person you'll want to keep permanently. Keep your notes from any previous auditions. Try to keep in loose contact with your second and third choices for each position.

Firing Musicians. Firing someone is always a sticky business, even when the separation is actually by mutual agreement.

To avoid creating disastrous situations, use some common sense. Never fire off the bandstand. If the player is absolutely too much for you to take one more minute, find an excuse to let him take the rest of the night off; fire him in the morning. Don't put yourself in the position of having an angry, unruly musician walking off the stage and through the audience, creating havoc for the rest of the band and your performance. The general rule is to never fire in anger. Wait until you've calmed down and can be professional and effective. Don't get personal and don't answer all the personal questions you're going to be asked. Stay businesslike and brief.

When firing someone it's wise to remember that you have a long life ahead of you. You don't want to say something you're going to regret later, and you don't want to make the musician look bad. It is never wise to burn your musicians behind you.

You may also have occasion to give a player advance notice of his termination. One of the things to realize when you give someone notice is that they have the right to look for work immediately and take the first thing that comes along, regardless of what it does to your schedule. Again, have a contingency plan for replacing this person as soon as possible.

The stickiest part about giving someone notice is that all of the problems he created will immediately disappear in his effort to change your mind. Don't go back on your decision. You'll invariably be sorry if you do.

Money and Taxes. There are a few basic rules about money that should be noted. First, at the club level, music is a cash business. If you aren't paid in cash by the club, cash their check at their bank. This is just common sense, but it's such a downfall for so many musicians that it is worth noting again. Don't assume that the club's check is good. Major corporate chains have been known to bounce checks. Small businesses may be run by nice guys who occasionally use their money twice. Always cash your check at the bank it was written on until you've played at the club for a few weeks and can feel secure about the employer's credit.

If you're the leader, it's nice to pay your people in cash. If you want a record of having paid out that money for your own tax records, have each musician sign a receipt. Otherwise, you may pay them by check after depositing the cash from the club in your account. (If you're getting a check from your leader, cash it at his bank.) If you deposit a check and it bounces, you'll be liable for the "nonsufficient fund" (NSF) charges. You'll have to cover with your own bank, cover with the people who you wrote checks to against the bad deposit, and go back to the original writer of the bad check to make it good. You may have to file in small claims court to get a judgment, and then you still may not get your money. A judgment means the court has decided you're owed the money; it doesn't possess any power of enforcement. To enforce a judgment on someone who won't pay up may require a lawyer, further court time, or a physically persuasive measure of your own discretion and imagination.

When you get beyond the club level you're no longer in a cash business. You're in a business requiring close financial attention. At that point, you should have an accountant, a business manager, or both to handle your finances. Always make sure that one of your people is at the ticket booth counting along with the theater's cashier to verify the number of customers. Always make sure that you are generally, if not intimately, aware of what money is coming in, what money is going out, where it's going to, and why. There are an amazing number of musicians who would be horrified at the thought of someone else tuning their axe, but who blithely allow some manager or business agent to take total financial control with only a vague or confusing explanation of what is taking place with the cash. Never forget that your money is both your interest and your responsibility. Stay aware of and involved with how that money is flowing in and going out.

As far as taxes go at the club level, the leader of the group receives the money in most situations and then pays the other players. This will show up on the I.R.S.'s records as the leader receiving a great deal of money. If you're the leader and want to protect yourself from paying taxes on all of that money, keep accurate records of how much was paid to you and how much you paid out to other musicians. Keep records of all the names and addresses of those musicians, in the event you get audited. If you have a Federal I.D. number, you'll have to file quarterly statements showing your projected income, expenses, and anticipated tax liability. If you don't use a Federal I.D. number, it might still be a good idea to keep records of all the Social Security numbers of the musicians you've paid over the year and send them all 1099 forms at the end of the year, showing how much you paid them. Copies of this form that you keep with your records will verify that the gross income from your music was reduced by wages paid to the other musicians. You can report only your portion on your taxes, or report the gross income and claim the deduction on an itemized form.

Consult an accountant if you find yourself in over your head. Hire an accountant or a business manager when you advance from the club phase to the more complicated stages of the business. It can be important to you as an individual who leads a band to safeguard your legal position by keeping accurate and specific records, because musicians are often suspected of not reporting all of their income.

Insurance Needs. There have been enough different laws passed in enough different states to confuse the issue of who is liable for equipment damaged onstage in a commercial establishment. As group leader, you should try to be aware of local regulations regarding club liability. There is no question, however, about who will suffer if the equipment is stolen, lost, or ruined while onstage or off. If you make music to make money you probably can't afford to be without your equipment for very long—say a day or two. On the road, loss of equipment can be devastating. You're the one who gets hurt.

Depending on where you live, the club owner may or may not be responsible for replacing your drum kit after a drunken brawl breaks it to pieces. No matter where you live, however, that club owner is under no obligation to let you keep the gig while you look around for the money to buy a new kit. If you are the leader of a group you are not responsible for your sidemen's damaged or stolen equipment unless you foolishly sign a contract saying you'll take that responsibility. But this doesn't mean you can't be sued anyway.

There are things you can do to avoid some of these problems. For a mere matter of handing over cash and having a current appraisal, you can buy an insurance policy to cover most if not all equipment emergencies. Make sure your stuff is covered by a replacement cost policy, that is, one based on what it would actually cost to replace the equipment. In some states you can even add professional musical equipment to your homeowner's or renter's insurance policy with an up-to-date appraisal on all items. Insist that the musicians in your group who have major amounts of equipment without duplication also carry insurance. If necessary, check to see if you can include them on your policy for the duration of your joint venture. Musicians who don't carry insurance or have duplicate backup equipment pose a real threat to your ability to continue on a smooth, steady course of work should some emergency or disaster occur.

Leverage

THE CONCEPT of leverage needs to be singled out and explained all by itself because it is the basis of movement or nonmovement in many aspects of life. Leverage is not control; it is a method of persuasion. Leverage is a force that must be recognized in every facet of the music business because each decision or nondecision that is made will be made because of someone's leverage. It is such a constant, everyday part of life that many people are never aware of the manipulations around them. To be successful in anything you must be aware of leverage. To control your musical career and understand what is happening and why, you have to be aware of at least three kinds of leverage: political, material, and monetary.

Political leverage translates into "who has the ear of the group and who can sway the group to do what he wants done." A band that is run by politics and not by a leader is very prone to factional alliances until the right combination of people with common desires and goals come together. Nevertheless, all groups have politics. Politics is the drummer who rushes and forgets where the head is coming off a solo, but can't be fired because the keyboard player is his best friend from grammar school. The drummer has political leverage. If the keyboard player is easily replaced, the drummer loses his leverage and both can be gotten rid of. If the keyboard player controls the group, you've got a problem.

Material leverage is "I own all the equipment" or "I own the club." If that keyboard player isn't utterly fantastic but owns the sound system, the speakers, and the three synthesizers that make your particular sound, he has material leverage that secures his position, thereby securing his friend the drummer's political leverage. And the beat goes on.

Monetary leverage is simple: "I got the gig; I signed the contract; I'm paying you."

Essentially, if you are in a position to make things go your way, you have leverage. If several people in the group have leverage, you have factional politics. This is like a Mexican standoff in an old cowboy movie—the first one to shoot had better be good. Actually, leverage is a lot like the loaded-gun theory: "I have a loaded gun and you don't; therefore, what I say goes." As with that theory, exercising the power can be potentially dangerous unless your power base is secure. 'Tis better to imply the power than to exert it; ergo, leverage.

Ignoring the fact of leverage or not taking it into account is one of the prime causes of failure at all levels of business life and, of course, in the music business. It must be recognized and handled professionally on the same level of importance as playing your instrument or singing. Everyone knows when power has been exerted, but only a few people recognize the presence and force of leverage. Be one of those people and you can make decisions more effectively.

It is crucial that you do make those decisions and not try to live with nondecisions. A nondecision is in and of itself a decision to let others rule, and by not deciding you will find that you have aligned yourself with the controlling faction by default. In a business situation, the old adage "You're either for me or against me" always applies—neutrality simply does not hold up. By not actively aligning yourself, you give impetus to the controlling faction (whoever that may be) and put yourself in jeopardy of being construed as an enemy or an unreliable quantity to be eliminated. This is especially true if there are any complaints about your performance (and don't be fooled—there are complaints about everyone's performance).

A FEW EXAMPLES OF LEVERAGE

A local group (here's a true story; the names have been changed to protect the guilty) became a house band at a nice, good-sized bar. The group consisted of drums, keyboards with left-hand bass (keys), lead guitar (lead), rhythm guitar (played by the leader), and a female vocalist who doubled on guitar and keys. Everyone but the drummer sang sometime during the night. The rhythm player made the contact, got the gig, had strong political ties with the owner, paid the group, and handed out the parts. In other words, this was a leadered band. He hired the other players, but because of their abilities and audience appeal they were never quite sidemen in the overshadowed sense of the word. In fact, the leader was the weakest part of the act: he often got drunk onstage, his singing was only adequate, and he played "air guitar" most of the night.

Factions arose. The female vocalist threatened to quit if the rhythm player wasn't replaced. The drummer and lead guitarist were solidly behind the rhythm player, as was the club owner with whom he maintained strong ties. The audience thought he was cute. The vocalist, who exerted her leverage of being the main draw, lost the fight and had to leave the group. The keyboard player, who was aligned with the vocalist, also left. The drummer and lead player remained, a new vocalist and keyboard player were brought in (this is a house band, remember; the gig is still secure), and life went on.

The rhythm player didn't get any better and no longer had the old vocalist and keyboard player to hide his faults. The drummer and lead player began to get disenchanted. The new keyboard player was heavily into drugs and was often useless or worse onstage. The loss that the group had suffered and the irritation of continuing problems brought about a new faction, whereby the drummer and lead player ousted the rhythm player and replaced him with a bass player to free up the keys. The old vocalist returned to the group, the owner accepted the change with some grumbling, and the gig remained secure. The rhythm player's leverage had been whittled down to being totally monetary, so he stopped payment on the drummer's and lead player's checks from his last week on the gig. They retaliated with legal action. He finally had to pay up.

Sound complicated and unbelievable? Look around; it happens every day. The rhythm player started off as the leader with political and monetary leverage; the vocalist had political leverage only. The vocalist chose to exercise her leverage and lost the battle. However, by leaving and opening the way for the keyboard player to leave, she made the rhythm player's faults more obvious, and thereby stripped him of his political alliances. They banded together to form a new alliance and ousted the rhythm player, who was then left with only monetary leverage. But monetary leverage doesn't work unless you are inside the situation, not outside. Furthermore, monetary leverage is only a bluff if there is legitimate legal recourse available to the opposing party. The rhythm player is sitting at home now, wondering what happened and why he's out of a job when it was his gig to begin with. He doesn't recognize the manipulation of leverage that cost him his job, or that his angry action with the checks cost him his reputation. He's since made the decision to drop out of the music business. This is wise; with his current reputation he can't find anyone who will work with him.

Another example: a high-class group of musicians form a marriage of convenience to play a well-connected club. The group consists of a drummer, keys with left-hand bass, and a guitar player. They play soft country-pop and old country and western. The guitar player is adamant about playing traditional C & W; the drummer wants more country-pop because the people like it. The keyboard player wants to hold the gig. They stay at the club for over a year, compromise on musical tastes, and gradually are given more nights and a budget to include a bass player. The bass player comes in recommended by the leader of another group that plays the same club on off nights. The bass player is a studio musician with major name connections, who just wants a place to "blow." He takes a dislike to the drummer at the first rehearsal and develops a faction with the guitarist who dislikes the drummer's taste and volume. Together they go to the owner of the club and demand that the drummer be replaced (this is after a full year of the drummer and guitar player working together four nights a week). The keys player, who is politically aligned with the drummer, does not exert his leverage for fear of losing his job; in other words, his power base is not secure. The drummer is replaced by a big-league studio drummer (recommended by the second group's leader) who goes out on tour after only one week and leaves a very weak replacement. The result: the gig becomes insecure for everyone because the quality of music has gone down. The other group moves into position to take over the four main nights. The original band is now in danger of losing what was one of the securest jobs in the area and will have to act quickly to protect their position, if they can.

What happened here? The keys player had a political alliance with the drummer, which could have amounted to one half of the band standing together. However, he decided not to interfere. This non-decision allowed the guitar and bass players to become an overruling force rather than just an opposing one. They were able to sway the owner to make a change that ended up putting everyone's job in jeopardy. The real leverage here was manipulated by the seemingly friendly and helpful leader of the second band, who encouraged the main-night group to change their winning hand, thereby weakening themselves enough to be challenged. Does this tactic sound familiar? It's the old "divide and conquer" routine you learned about in high-school history. It still works. The main-night band now has to fight for its position. The second group gets the chance to take the bulk of the week away from them.

How could this disaster have been avoided? By the partnership not allowing a new partner to join the group if he didn't work well with all the original members; by the keyboard player exercising his leverage as a factional ally of the drummer; by finding out more about the replacement drummer than that he's a good player; by realizing the fact of the second leader's manipulation; by a group confrontation to talk out problems.

A note: direct confrontation is one of the most effective counterbalances to the exertion of leverage. And that means direct confrontation of everyone in the group at the same time. Small, secret meetings only lead to extended soap operas. Again, leverage and the manipulation of leverage are what will control your career. Learn to recognize it; learn to develop it; learn to exercise it and defend against it prudently.

The Career Plan

IN ORDER to go somewhere, you must know where you want to go. It also helps to have some idea of how to get there. In the music business, this is no easy task because there are no surefire ways of getting anywhere, except out of the business. One of the best ways to proceed, therefore, is to think backward from where you want to be. That's not as hard as it sounds, but it does take sitting down and planning a little. Start with a five-year plan.

Here's an example: in five years you want to have a hit album and be playing major concerts.

Now think backward. Before you have a hit album, you'll need several hit singles to make up the album. Also, you'll need to be worthy of being on a major concert tour. Therefore, you might plan first to be an opening act for a major name.

Before anyone will let you open for them, you'll have to have a strong, proven stage show. You'll need a strong audience that follows you from club to club (or from showcase to showcase, if applicable) and buys your promotional materials (records, T-shirts, and bumper stickers). It will also be helpful to have been written up in the local papers and have captured the attention of the corporate music industry through a good word-of-mouth reputation. Before a major label picks you up for national or international distribution of your singles, you may have to press on an independent label or even produce a vanity press record to sell off the stage.

Before you can attract press and industry attention, your product will have to be noteworthy. So you'll have to create a successful showcase or club group with a unique style or good writing. You should be able to attract a loyal audience and garner financial backing and an active support group.

Before you can be successful, you'll have to enlist the right group of musicians and vocalists with at least competent abilities, a professional attitude, a great deal of desire, future-oriented thinking, adaptability, and an insurmountable, irrepressible resistance to rejection.

Therefore, a basic five-year plan might be the following:

1. Form the group with the right people.

2. Develop a good show with good music and either a unique style or very fine original material. Gather or hire a support group and find financial backing.

3. Develop a local-and-beyond following with good press coverage and a good word-of-mouth reputation. Attract the attention of the corporate music industry, including record companies and their A&R (artists and repertoire) people. Promote and sell your own line of band products.

4. Cut a single or an album either on an independent label or through a vanity press. Sell the record off the stage, get local airplay, and at least local distribution. Find a major-name act that you can open for. Find a major label for your future recording projects with national and international distribution.

5. Put out a string of hits from a single album or series of albums. Develop enough of a national following through your recordings to warrant your own concert tour.

This is, of course, only one very general scenario that can be developed after setting the goal of a hit album and concert tour. Since there are no guarantees in the music business, no tried-and-true-this-always-works method that can be followed again and again, any plan that you make will have to be tailored to the individuals in the group, their joint long-term goals, and the finances and support you have or feel you can attract. Certainly, any plan you draw up should be realistic in its timetable and well matched to your abilities and resources. But striving for a little bit more than you think you can accomplish might just give you the push you need to go over the top.

Without a plan, you won't even be sure what the top is. After all, is your goal to make your living from music for the rest of your life? Or is it to go for stardom and drop out if you don't make it? Do you want to do live performances or just record? Do you want to be a "faceless" band or an individual name? Would you be happy with local celebrityhood, or is your passion for music just a stepping stone to some other form of entertainment, such as acting? The important point is to set a specific goal, then work backward. Figure out where you want to be just before you hit that goal, where you want to be before that, and so on, until you're down to your current level. Then begin to work toward the next level up in specific terms, and take it one step at a time. You'll be able to know whether you're really moving up by comparing your current position to your projected position.

Circumstances and opportunities will probably cause you to readjust your plan as you go along, but having a specific guideline to fall back on can keep you from wallowing at the same level for too long with the delusion that you are accomplishing something concrete. Many groups manage to convince themselves that they're going somewhere when they're actually not advancing at all. It's much easier to accomplish a specific goal, albeit a stepping stone, than to just randomly "reach for the top."

PICKING A NAME

Volumes have been written on picking the right name, and it is without a doubt one of the most agonizing decisions that a group has to make. In reality, the name means more to you than to anyone else; honestly it does. Pick any name. If you become famous, the name will be remembered. If you don't become famous, it won't be because of the name you picked.

Try not to use names that will get you sued, such as "Xerox" or "The Who." If another group is using the same name (as is often the case with any good name), the question will eventually boil down to a matter of legal right: which party has legally protected that name.

You can trademark your name, after doing a reasonable search, on either the federal or state level. It is not very expensive and can save you untold aggravation later on. For information on how to institute a search and trademark your name, contact the United States Department of Commerce, Patent and Trademark Office, Commissioner of Patents and Trademarks, Washington, DC 20231.

If another group has their name legally protected, you'll probably have to change yours. You can try to challenge them in court. You'll have to prove that they haven't publicly used the name or that your stature in the industry is significantly greater than theirs. It's very risky, but you may end up being able to use the name, or at least not having to pay damages.

But be forewarned: major acts will pay ridiculous prices to bury a group that is an irritant so that there are no later problems. This is true even if yours is the protected name and theirs is not. It has to be recommended, therefore, that when you get serious about a name, you take all legal steps available to protect yourself, regardless of the cost, and realize that there are no guarantees. In the final analysis, it is wiser to spend two hundred dollars protecting your name than to have to forfeit what could amount to millions later. Again, the name itself is not the important issue—it's who has the legal right to exploit that name that matters.

Gearing for Success

AFTER YOU'VE found a name, determined your group's current level, and identified your next immediate goal, you'll need to know about some of the compromises necessary to reach that goal. In your tour through the music business you'll be working in a variety of situations, from clubs and concerts to recording studios, each with its own set of expectations and required skills. The attitude you have in a club, for instance, will be different from the way you handle a concert; a recording studio will demand yet another set of compromises. It will be important for you to be able to adapt to the special requirements of each setting—to be able to shift your perspective as you move from one to the other. You'll also be dealing with people of all kinds, beginning with the audience and including personnel at record companies. It is vital that you be able to adapt to the needs of these people. This may not be easy, especially when their expectations turn out to be different from your own. Here's where the compromise comes into play. Achieving success in the music business usually means balancing your own needs as a musician against the needs and desires of the public, the operator, the agents, or the record companies, each requiring a different compromise. Compromising is difficult for some, impossible for others. The trick is to put yourself in the other person's shoes so you can figure out what they want, as opposed to what you want to give them.

Most musicians know what they want to do with their music and often get rather pugnacious about their right to say with their music what they want to say the way they want to say it, regardless of what agents, owners, or the audience appear to want. Groups that have worked hard to get their special sound tend to become family-tight and rationalize everything from the inside, not allowing outside influences to have an impact. As a result, they end up with an overriding attitude of "My way, right or wrong" when it comes to any kind of change or modification of the band's sound or presentation. It is true that there have been numerous bands and artists with this somewhat obstinate attitude—choosing to go their own way even if it takes years for the public to appreciate what they're doing—that have indeed waited out the tide of public opinion and "made it big" when their turn came. But let's face it, this is not the norm.

Every musician wants to believe that his will be the group to turn the industry around to good music—in other words, the kind of music his group plays. In reality, much of this obstinate faith is merely standing in the way of commercial success, especially when the faith is misplaced or the view is out of focus. To be successful on any level, there has to be a happy meeting between the musician's subjective, aesthetic opinion and audience appeal. It's very difficult to judge your own work and very easy to be led into a false sense of security by club audiences or groupies. Eventually, you'll have to get an objective opinion about your music that is both professionally sound and from a source that you will believe and respect. But before you get to the point where you want to subject yourself to that kind of scrutiny, start to learn about some of the compromises necessary to make your band viable.

THE CLUB

In the clubs, an initial compromise must be reached between what the musicians want, what the audience wants, and what the operator or club owner wants. On the club level, agents aren't particularly important. This much is obvious: any group that does not take into consideration what the audience wants has limited itself to a permanent position at the bottom of the heap. It's also rather obvious that a group that isn't aware of what the operator wants will not keep gigs. Moreover, to disregard the musician's needs is a good way to ensure frequent personnel changes, which are the bane of advancement.

This kind of compromise requires a highly professional attitude. In a club, you have to play the room, making the sale of the room more important than the sale of the band. You can accomplish this by having the audience, the bar personnel, the operator, and the band be involved in making a success. The band really becomes like an employee-extension of the club. Promote the menu from the stage, advertise any specialties, point out the waitresses and bar people by name. Get the audience to feel like a part of the room and let the club people know you're working for their benefit. In a club, as in any venture, there are only two attitudes: good and bad. If you don't have a good attitude about where you're working and about the people, services, and products offered there, then you will come off as having a bad attitude. This will be picked up by the people in the room and will ultimately result in less than success, to say the least. This is one of the reasons why a good band that "everybody loves" can get notice for no apparent reason. It's not that they do anything wrong; it's just that they don't do the important things right.

THE STUDIO

Studio decisions require that you keep in mind the musicians' creative needs and the overall audience appeal of the product that you are creating, as well as the intentions of the songwriter and the needs and desires of the potential buyer, who is not the audience but the industry representative. Generally, the personnel on a recording does not have to be the same as the club personnel you work with, unless you are trying to advertise the group over the specific tunes.

A studio product should be handled as a separate tool in and of itself. All decisions should support the creation of a successful product, achieving an equal balance between artistic considerations and commercial requirements. Studio products usually fall into one of three categories: cover tunes played to illustrate a band's ability and saleability; original tunes to illustrate a band's writing prowess and potential for creating hits; original tunes to illustrate the saleability of those tunes to other artists.

If you're recording cover tunes, you want to keep in mind, in a general way, what an operator or an agent would like to hear. The actual audience will never hear this kind of tape and, therefore, should not be given high priority. On an originals tape made to show off the band's writing and hit potential (this could also be a product that is submitted to a label or is vanity pressed) your criteria must include audience appeal, the band's input and special sound, and the buyer's needs and desires. If you go into the studio thinking that you're going to lay down what you want to lay down and forget what the industry people want, then you can do just that: forget the industry, because it will certainly forget you. If your product is specifically meant to sell your original music to other artists, then audience appeal, writer's desires, and industry (target artist) needs take total precedence over musician's expression, unless it coincides with audience appeal and writer's desires.

Again, as with the rest of your projects to further your career, you must be aware of what is needed, have a specific goal or formula in mind, and use your time carefully. Remember—all studio decisions should be made outside the studio, before the clock starts ticking off money.

CONCERTS

By the time you get to the concert level, all major decisions will be handled on a money level. This will take into consideration the artistic performance, geared to audience appeal and industry needs, you have built up to this point. (It is pretty obvious that you cannot use the same act on a concert stage that you used in a five-night-a-week club, just as it should be obvious that the intensity necessary for a concert will not work in the clubs.) Few groups or individual artists can afford to finance their own concerts, nor is it economically advantageous to do so. The production of a concert is for the purpose of making money and should be handled by people who understand that arena and its profit requirements. This is true regardless of your personal reasons for playing the concert, which may include advertisement of your record or promotion of your group. Therefore, the decisions that you as an artist will make in a concert situation, such as tune selection and staging, should have already evolved during the process of reaching the concert level or will be dictated by financial resources and the needs of the producers or promoters.

THE AUDIENCE

First, remember that what you'd want to see and hear when you go to a club or show is not the same as what an audience or operator wants. Your tastes are colored by your knowledge and abilities. The audience has no stage knowledge or experience, and no professional musical abilities. They come to be entertained, not to listen to you play your songs, although at the concert level these should be one and the same.

Before you can attract a specific audience that follows you from show to show, you have to find out what it is that entertains a club clientele. You can ask the people sitting out there what they want, but their answers will not be truthful. That's because they'll tell you only what they think they'd like, rather than what they really *feel* would be worth paying for another drink to hear. Members of an audience are not obligated to separate out their true desires from their surface thoughts for your benefit. There are a few ways to decide what any given audience wants. One is to use trial and error. This requires a widely varied repertoire and a good deal of time, which you may not be given. Another way is to take the advice of the bar personnel (not necessarily the operator) about the groups that did good business in the room before you. The best way is to have intimate knowledge of the room; to have seen for yourself what has worked and what hasn't worked for past groups; to know the regulars, semiregulars, and bar personnel; and be part of their crowd before you ever play the room. Having an intimate relationship with your audience is the first step to success in any room. When you get onstage, the customers are already pulling for you, the bar personnel already feel you are one of them, and these various factions all contribute to a successful engagement.

THE OPERATOR

Knowing what an operator or club owner wants can be tricky. He wants to make money, of course, but how much does he want to make? Find out on a nightly basis what your sales quota is; after all, you are working in the club to promote his sales. Does he want an SRO (standing room only) crowd or a turnover crowd? Does he want to make his money with a specific image or just with whatever sells? Is he trying to develop a younger clientele or attract older, more monied customers? What atmosphere does he want maintained? Talk to the operator. Get specific answers if you can. Talk to his right-hand aides and his bar manager. Know what you're working with and for. Every operator or owner has a regular or two who is a friend. Talk to the friend. Become a friend of the friend. Get him in your corner; make a political tie. The music business is people. Know how the operator wants to make his money and how much he wants to make and you'll have a much better chance of delivering. You can't deliver the right product if you don't know what the right product is.

AGENTS AND MANAGERS

When you're working in the clubs, try not to drive yourself crazy about what the local agents want. An agent wants whatever he can sell right now. His perspective is way out of focus with yours, because his main concern is not that you work, but that he gets a commission. You can easily follow an agent's every dictum and never work. Keep your own perspective. An agent doesn't hire you; he doesn't pay you; he doesn't buy your records and T-shirts; he doesn't put up money for your demos; and he doesn't cover your union dues. He loses no money if the gig falls through.

Club agents will try to convince you that they can make or break you, but most of them can't. A good agent with connections can sell the product you have made yourself into, but he won't help you develop into that product. If you're working on the road, an agent can smooth things out for you by keeping your schedule full, but he can also leave you high and dry if something breaks down in that schedule. An agent without connections can only scrape for work as your representative. He will sell whomever he can to any buyer he finds because his commission on somebody, not necessarily you, is his main concern. The expense that he incurs to keep his business going makes this attitude necessary.

A manager, on the other hand, who is specifically trying to advance your career, will not impose any personal opinions on you unless he honestly believes that those opinions reflect an industry or audience requirement. Of course, this refers to a good, reputable manager. Always check out the people you are planning to rely on through every means possible: your union, the Better Business Bureau, the police department, local and national magazine editors or publisher's reps, and other managers who have or specifically have not done business with them.

The music industry is a moneymaking business, and an awful lot of cash changes hands from hopeful musicians to unethical managers, agents, record companies, producers, publishers, and promoters who talk well and deliver poorly. Try to look at any offer you get from the point of view of the person or organization who is offering it. What do they really get out of the deal? What do you really get out of the deal? What really is the deal after all the fancy talk is done and the actual agreement is on paper? If it doesn't look like they're going to get much out of any deal that is being offered to you, then you're probably being suckered for more than you realize.

RECORD COMPANIES

Major-label record companies with international distribution networks want something they can get excited about and can use to make a major profit. It is expected that a good percentage of the products they commit to will turn out to be failures, which translates into tax losses—a necessary and profitable transaction for many businesses today. Most companies will, however, go into a new venture with the knowledge that it may fail, but with the hope that it won't.

Major labels want something just like what's on the radio right now, only slightly different or better. Independent labels want something that will push them into the major leagues. Innovation is largely self-financed, then picked up and copied. To know what any particular company wants, you must know the company. How many divisions does it have? What different types of music does it record and sell? Who is under contract to it; how many albums have they done with the company; and what has been the focus of those albums? Whom do you need to impress in the company? What does it take to impress him? What new groups has the company signed in the last year? What kind of focus do those groups have? Do you fit into that category?

How do you find out all these things? Call the company. Talk to the secretaries, to the public relations department, and to the A&R men. Go to the library and do some research in the trade papers. Make a friend in the company. Find out who your target is and what your target wants and see if you can give it to him. If you can't, look for another company. If you're making a studio product or giving a showcase performance with the idea in mind that "maybe somebody from a record company will hear me" and you don't know specifically what companies to aim for and what they want, you're essentially firing a shotgun into the sky with the hope that one of the pellets will hit a bird that you'll want to eat.

It all boils down to research and salesmanship: know whom you have to impress; know what it takes to impress them; know what you have to offer; then juggle it all. It's complicated at the club level. It's more complicated at the recording level. It can be very costly in money and time at all levels, so research before you audition, before you record, before you submit your material, and before you ask for financing. Did you think this business was about playing music?

OTHER BUSINESS CONTACTS

Besides all the people who are directly related to your career (agents, operators, players, and audience), there is a group of people on the outskirts of the industry who can indirectly help or hinder your everyday working career. It is important to recognize these people. It is also important not to alienate them or disregard their significant contributions. Musicians who have not yet realized what really goes on in the music business have a tendency to regard people on the fringes of the business as dilettantes of little consequence or even, in the cases of ex-musicians, as laughable has-beens. This is a mistake. Although these people are not hireable, steady support people, they are intermittently active musical aficionados who may have a great deal of knowledge and/or influence in their particular field of interest. Never disregard the potential strength of someone who has been hanging onto the fringe of this business for any length of time.

How do you identify these people? To start with, pay attention to the people who get talked about in the bar or in the area. Be aware of popular, nonprofessional attractions, such as the former guitarist for a heavy name who retired and now just "sits in" a lot. Everyone seems to love his performances, but he doesn't get paid and won't take a contracted gig. He's an important sit-in who is established but part-time, or a former professional, probably with contacts. He's a good person to become friendly with; certainly he isn't the kind of guy to antagonize.

Technically oriented people who buy, service, sell, or rent equipment and services on a part-time basis as a hobby or side interest are also good people to know and to have on your side. Besides the obvious benefit of using their services when needed, their enthusiasm for this particular field of interest can be a windfall for you if they can turn you onto good equipment deals, or teach you intricacies of your electronic gear that you would never have considered without being shown. Such people can be an invaluable aid to a career for which they develop a personal affinity.

Another source of helpful personnel are the local colleges, filled with students and faculty members who are highly trained and eager to get onstage. In a club frequented by this kind of crowd, occasionally inviting a student or teacher to jam enhances your rapport with the regular audience. When handled correctly, these young musicians and well-established teachers can serve as a positive political force.

Usually they are happy to let you tell them when they can sit in, and they are reasonably flexible onstage. They can provide an occasional addition to the depth of sound on the bandstand without the expense of an additional player. They can also be a handy resource for emergency replacement situations.

One more type of person to pay attention to is the "casual people broker." He makes deals and person-to-person connections that bring musicians together with equipment, producers, other musicians, and gigs. He is not as easy to spot as the other kinds of fringe personalities, but you'll find him in the shadows of many well-established bands or local celebrity groups.

The main point to keep in mind is that most of these people will not go out of their way to hinder your career unless you give them a reason to. At the same time, most of them will not go out on a limb to *help* your career unless it is worth their while. It could be worth their while if you have established a personal bond with them, or if they stand to gain something that they want, not necessarily money. With such people, satisfying a personal interest is often more important than getting a financial return.

A Support Group

A SUPPORT GROUP is people: people who are not performers; people who believe in you; people who will actively support you with money, publicity, contacts, physical help, or any other kind of assistance. The operative word here is "actively." A group of fans who show up at your performances but cannot help you pay for your demo tape or walk into an office to convince an executive of your worth do not provide active support. They aren't helping you to develop your career. They simply make up your audience.

It is important to have both a loyal audience and an active support group. In the 1980s, it isn't enough to go to an A&R man and say "Hey, we're a great group." Individual confidence is necessary, but insufficient. You need a spokesman who is not part of your performing group who believes in you and can make connections, help you with your research, put money behind you or find money to put behind you, and run interference for you when it's necessary—in other words, put himself on the line for you. The powers-that-be, whoever they are in your particular case, will be more easily convinced of your viability if you've already got an active, vocal representative who is excited about you. Businessmen like to do business with other businessmen, not with artists. Businessmen will "catch" the excitement about a new product (you) much faster from someone else who is also excited about the product, than from the product itself. Music is a business; you are a product; art is something you put on the wall. If your desire is to play your songs and to hell with commercial considerations, why are you reading this book? You need a sales force—a support group.

Beyond these practical matters, there is the additional fact that no group can sustain confidence and vitality without outside support and encouragement. This is another function of your support group: to intertwine its future with your future, thereby giving you a life raft of self-credibility for times when the going gets rough and nothing seems to be moving forward.

How to Get a Support Group

Support groups can either be gathered or bought. Your first support group will probably consist of your family and friends. They may or may not be as actively involved as you need them to be. As your performance gathers strength, seek out strong fans who can be relied upon to handle important tasks with which you need help. Gathering a support group can be a long, tedious process. On the other hand, you may hit a pocket of people who are looking for a new adventure into the glamorous world of show business.

Buying a support group isn't always as easy as it sounds. No good, reputable agent or manager can help your career unless he is excited about you, so first you have to be an exciting prospect. You'll need your stage show, your musical ideas, and your dedicated personnel all in place before it will be worth a professional's while to put himself on the line for you.

You may find that you go through several phases of support people in the process of climbing your personal success ladder. This isn't necessarily unusual or detrimental. Just be careful that you don't burn any bridges with the people you leave behind, because you may find yourself in a less advantageous situation farther down the line. Pay attention to the reasons that one person drops out or another joins up. Is it truly because you have outgrown their abilities? Or is it because you've used up their enthusiasm? Are you attracting people who really want to put you over the top, or people who just want to garner some personal glory from their connection with a popular musical act? Are you fooling them or are they fooling you? Hopefully, nobody's fooling anybody and you're all committed to the same goal. That's a step in the direction of success.

The Female Performer

THE PROBLEMS of being female in the music business are rarely discussed. When people do talk about them, they manage to reach few agreements. Let's face it: music is a sexist business. Whether you decide that it's getting better or believe that it'll never change, you can't deny that music is a field of show business in which women are vastly outnumbered and rarely encouraged. It also happens to be the field in which a woman can shine the brightest if she manages to fight her way to the top.

Some irritating but undeniable facts hold true: most women who succeed in the music business do so as singers; most (but not all) female groups lose public interest quickly; most big-name rock and pop female artists transmute their careers to include acting as quickly as possible. The advantages and disadvantages that women have in the music business are subtle but crucial, and it is important to be aware of the realities if you're going to rationally plan a career.

A FEMALE'S DISADVANTAGES

▶ From a strictly physical point of view, more of your commercial viability is dependent on age and beauty than is a man's. This is a deeply rooted problem that women are fighting in the offices, but cannot as easily combat onstage. Audiences like to look at pretty people, and the definition of a pretty female is young and thin with a beautiful face, beautiful hair, and nice legs. After the age of twenty-seven or twenty-eight you're not considered young anymore. Audiences look at you as a woman who has been at it for awhile and still hasn't made it. The thirty-three-year-old man who plays the clubs is "getting seasoned." The thirty-three-year-old woman who still plays the clubs "used to be really something." There are exceptions to this rule, of course, most notably in country music and gospel where women rather than girls are popular.

▶ Musical standards are not applied to women in the same way as they are to men. As a musician, you have to be better than good, or sexually connected to another band member. Your political leverage is always somewhat in doubt because it is assumed that any female player can be easily replaced. As a vocalist, you have to fit a preconceived sound that appeals to the men in the group. Even in an all-female situation, old attitudes die hard and you may find yourself subjected to similar narrow expectations.

▶ Male musicians in general feel uneasy about working with female musicians. The musical stage is very "macho." This state of affairs can be traced back to early Greek theater, in which all roles—including female parts—were played by men in masks. Many female musicians who have outstanding ability still get only grudging respect and run the risk of being replaced by a lesser-talented male simply because he's "easier to work with." Men are hesitant about being onstage with women because women "think differently." Even the most enlightened, liberated man doesn't particularly like working with women in a situation where the name of the game is "Hey, look at me." A woman is natural competition for the audience's attention.

▶ Club owners may insist that there be a female front, then discount her contribution. As a vocalist, you may be expected to sing almost every song for five hours a night, five nights a week, then be replaced if you start to lose your energy on the fifth night. Females on a traditionally nonfemale instrument such as horn, lead guitar, or drums can often turn out to be only a novelty attraction that loses appeal when the novelty wears off. A female horn player who is every bit as good as the male players she's working with may find that people aren't believing their ears and don't think she's all that good, simply because they can't adjust to the idea of a woman playing the horn.

▶ Often band members, men in the audience, and operators assume that any female onstage is fair game and should pay for the privilege of being allowed to perform. If you don't agree, labels like "bitch" and "prima donna" don't do much to help your career.

Are you thoroughly discouraged? Well, don't be. These may be the realities of working in the clubs, but a musically talented female can take the same rules, turn them into advantages, and play the game any way she likes.

A FEMALE'S ADVANTAGES

▶ Any female performer can take the stage away from a group of men, simply by virtue of being female, if she has the right attitude. People like to look at women. While a female might have trouble getting hired into a group if she's not young and pretty, she can always put her own act together. The trick is to not let the negatives you experience or hear make you feel bitter or cowed. Approach each performance with a "this is my audience and I love them" attitude, and the audience will usually respond in kind, no matter what your age or basic appearance, no matter what antics the men pull.

▶ People like to hear female voices. They're pretty. They're sexy. They're soothing and reassuring like Mommy's voice. It's a natural "in." An audience would rather hear an average female singer do a love song than an average male singer. Three-voice female vocal acts have long been an industry standard—one that has proven to have tremendous staying power.

▶ Today, many club bands cannot work unless they include a female. Operators find that their receipts go up when a woman is onstage. Women are moneymakers because their very presence implies sex, and sex (as advertising has proven) sells everything. This position gives any female a built-in element of leverage.

▶ All-female groups with a good stage show and good music can bypass male groups on the upward career ladder because of their inherent novelty and strong audience/sex appeal. Male groups with female members on instruments or vocals may be able to open new doors by promoting the women as a strength of the band, thereby creating the fact from the illusion.

▶ Individual female artists stand a better chance of gathering a support system than individual male artists. Why? Because of sex appeal, because women are more "glamorous" than men, because men like to support women in show business and will think of their efforts in more personal, less businesslike terms than with a male artist. Also, the industry searches for female stars. Although a man can anticipate a longer-lasting career in the spotlight as a general rule, women can diversify more easily and generate enormous financial return.

MAKING THE MOST OF YOUR GENDER

First, be aware that you are selling sex, whether you want to or not, whether it's blatant or subtle. Use that fact as a tool to develop your audience appeal. A woman can be as extreme as she wants, from the soft, feminine approach to wild and gritty, from a "one of the boys" attitude to the "boy toy" image. A woman can look like anything she wants to onstage, as long as she has the band's support to pull it off. In this case, the group that you work with becomes part of your support group. If you're as heavy as Mama Cass Elliott and your band can create an image around that, you've got one more chip on the winning side. The fact is that the band's image will be the image that you as a female portray, so decide on your individual characterization early and then build the group around it.

Firm, specific goals and career plans are essential for female artists who want to do more than play the clubs for a few years, then settle down to a family. A strong support group that includes musicians, financial backers, and business representatives is also essential and should be developed as quickly as possible. Most successful female artists have or have had male backing and male efforts behind them. Use this to your advantage. If you have a strong female support system, let the novelty of the situation show through. Don't try to pretend you're doing business as usual. Learn how to turn all the negatives that are thrown at you into positives, and work quickly. Don't try to fit the "jack-of-all-trades-master-of-none" image that many male musicians effect. Rather, get very good at your particular axe, whether instrumental or vocal, and expand from there. Realize that you may have to branch out into acting or dancing or to readjust yourself to a different style of music. Prepare yourself for future career moves.

There is no good reason why a strong female artist shouldn't be able to shift from group to group and from club to club over a lifelong musical career, as so many male musicians do. Reality, however, proves that this will seldom occur. At some nebulous point in her thirties, a woman will drift out of the music business if she hasn't advanced beyond the neighborhood club level. Marriage, children, and a desire to eat regularly are all factors influencing a decision to drop out. Be aware of this trap when you get started in the business and make plans for your musical future even if you don't make it out of the clubs. A female who performs as a single, for example, can get work more easily than a male single simply because she's female. Use this fact to your advantage and make sure you are competent on a solo instrument. (This will enhance your current viability, too.) If you are primarily an instrumentalist, make sure that you can sing enough to get by. If your instrument is not a solo one, learn a second axe; you may need it later. You can have the same chance as any man at a lifelong musical career if you are a realist from the start.

Be wary of alliances built on sex, but if you do decide to establish leverage by such means, keep your options fluid enough that you don't lose ground when your lover does. Don't let male musicians con you into being the "mommy" of the group, for example, taking care of them when they get sick or helping them with their personal problems. Confidences shared with you by a male performer during a lapse can be cause enough to replace you later. Use what you have at your disposal, rather than be used for what you've got.

Expect to have your abilities, morals, and alliances questioned regularly. Don't let it affect you. Expect to have to sustain your position through means other than your original talents, such as writing, acting, outrageous concert performances, or joining a corporate band situation. Don't let that deter you. As in any other aspect of life, to be successful in the music business as a female you will have to be twice as good, three times as strong, unbelievably determined, and willing to put up with rude and derogatory attitudes. You will need a strong support group, a stronger constitution, and the ability to accomplish faster than your male counterparts. Remember, though, that another term for top female entertainers who are called bitchy, talentless, cold, egocentric, or snotty is successful.

2

THE MUSIC

The foundation of your career is music. You'll be drawing from two basic sources for your performing material: songs that you or your band members write, and songs that are taken from the radio or recordings. Writing songs is an excellent way to make money from your art, apart from getting paid as a performer. You receive royalties for recordings of your song that are manufactured and distributed, and for performances of the song on the radio or TV. Songwriting may also fulfill your need for personal expression, and help your band find its special sound. Your group may also pick up other composers' songs from the radio or records. The process of learning popular or standard tunes will help you develop musical technique, and is a basic step toward building a commercial performance repertoire.

Writing Songs

SONGWRITING DOESN'T lend itself to easy rules. You can learn formulas for creating rhymes or chord progressions, but translating those formulas into a hit song involves a lot of creativity and abstract theory. If you can sit down and write words, music, or both in a coherent form that expresses what you want it to, then you don't have to worry about fitting your work into specific formulas. You have to worry about general guidelines that will make your writing more communicative and more recognizable—in short, more saleable.

Not everyone can write. If you don't have something to say or any idea of how to say it, you may not be a writer. If you want to be a writer and don't know where to start, try taking your ten favorite songs, writing out the lyrics and chord progressions, and studying the forms. You'll probably find patterns that you can follow with words and chords of your own.

There are several ways of writing tunes:

Write lyrics first, then music.

Write music first, then lyrics.

Write words and music together.

Try to fit bits and pieces of both together.

Everyone has their own formula for success, but unless you're writing instrumental-only tunes, it is often helpful to write the lyrics before you tackle the music.

LYRICS

Lyrics (words) are usually comprised of verses, a chorus, and an optional bridge. Verses either tell a story, paint an image, or describe an emotion. If the main thrust of the song is in the chorus, the verses have to supply support for that chorus. If the main thrust of the song is in the verse, the chorus should be a summary or wrap-up. Either way, get to the point immediately, then expand or restate. Unless you're writing a comedy song, don't try to build suspense by slowly leading up to the main thrust. If you check through your favorite songs, you'll find that those with the thrust in the verse usually begin with the verse. Those songs in which the chorus contains the main point usually start with the chorus. That gets the point of the song across right away and lets the rest of the tune support and expand it.

It's unfortunate that so many Americans were graded in school according to the quantity rather than quality of what they wrote and were given assignments to turn out five hundred words on the Great Wall of China or twelve pages on "What I Did on My Summer Vacation." When you're writing a song, it's important to say as much as you feel you want to say, then stop. Don't make up a third or fourth verse if you don't have anything to say in a third or fourth verse. The difference will show.

If you want to write a song and can't think of what to write about, try writing a love song. There are almost endless variations on the love song theme: boy loves girl; boy loses girl; boy and girl reunite; boy and girl are happy together forever; love is a beautiful thing; the loneliness of your lover far away; daddy loves baby, to name a few. Most top 40, country, rock, jazz, and R&B tunes—in other words, most tunes—are about love. Another popular topic in song lyrics is dancing, which you do to kill time and have fun while you're looking for someone to fall in love with.

Songs about social issues no longer have the forum that the sixties provided, but they do enjoy surges of popularity every few years. Be aware of the times that you're living in and what the trends of the social protests are. The problem with relevant tunes is that they become dated within a few months, if not weeks. They need to be put on vinyl and distributed quickly in order to be effective and timely.

Songs that use shock words or words that might be repugnant or disturbing to large segments of the population may be fast hits, but probably will not become "standards," or sustained hits that become remakes every few years, and that will provide you with continuing royalties.

Good lyrics don't have to be profound or sophisticated. They do have to be ear-catching, easily understood words that the average person on the street can relate to. Lyrics don't have to read well. Don't make the mistake so many new songwriters do—writing for readability on paper as opposed to writing for the ear. Lyrics don't have to be grammatically correct; they have to sound good out loud. They have to make sense to a stranger. They have to seem familiar to the listener, even at the first hearing. Try not to couch your message in poetry. Lyrics are not poetry, although there have been many cases of poems put to music. Use recognizable words and easily understood phrases. A point to remember: repetition of a line (the hook) is not only acceptable but expected. Redundancy, on the other hand, is boring.

Probably the most important part of a commercial song is the hook. The hook can start the song, start or end the chorus, end the verses, or be used in any combination of the above. Make the hook easy to understand with small syllable words. Use word play, twists on common clichés, summarizing comments, or any phrase that rolls off the tongue easily and is memorable after one hearing. Keep it reasonably short and plan to name the tune after the hook. Make sure it is the main point of the tune, lyrically.

The only place that the hook usually doesn't show up is in the bridge. Most songs today have a bridge of some sort, besides the verse and chorus. Since the bridge is, by definition, a musical change-up or transition, the lines do not have to be of the same texture, length, or sequence type as the rest of the song. Two to four lines is the norm for an effective bridge. It should be the final extension of the lyrical idea of the song, like an extra added attation.

Another thing you'll probably find in most of your favorite tunes is a two-way idea. For example, the boy tells the girl how he feels about her, then tells her how she acts toward him. If you're telling a story about something you did, give someone else's point of view or reaction, or tell about a consequence of the deed. If you're painting an image, use a comparison or a contrast, too.

It is important to remember that none of these guidelines are carved in granite. Since songwriting is such a personal art and requires abstract creation, you'll have to adjust and adapt the rules and formulas as you work with them. The more tunes you write, the easier it will be to develop your own formulas. The average rule of thumb is that for every five songs you write, one will be good; for every five good tunes you write, one will be saleable. Again, this rule doesn't always apply; it depends on your abilities and stage of development. Songwriting is a lifelong learning process.

Music

In a good song, the lyrics and the music should complement each other. They should live and work side-by-side in a mutually supportive partnership. "Music" in this sense refers to melody, chords, and rhythm—the basic compositional elements. Added harmonies, instrumentation, and signal processing are part of the arrangement and production, and should also support the overall feeling of the tune.

Every musician has his own method of working, so the decision to write a melody first or build a chord structure first is totally up to you and the particular tune you're working on. Modern music ranges from the incredibly simple to the sophisticated to the intricate, but the key element in most saleable tunes is the flow and groove of the music. A lot of that has to do with how you put all the pieces together.

Whether you come up with a potential hit depends a lot on your ability to create a musical hook. This might be a guitar riff, a bass line, a drum pattern or, more typically, a catchy vocal line that can be repeated. Most hit singles have some sort of musical hook. A good exercise is to listen to tunes on the radio and see if you can pick out the hook in each one.

Melodies can be created in a number of different ways. The first method is to hear a melody in your head and write it down or sing it into a tape recorder to preserve it. If you have a creative mind and can be sure that what you're "hearing" is original and not an old melody from some forgotten song, this can be one of the best ways of writing. Another way is to use your instrument to find notes and rhythms that work with already written lyrics. This is largely a matter of inspired trial and error, but can yield good results if you work at it and don't accept just any results.

Another method that can produce a good tune, but is rather risky if not used properly, is to take an existing melody and alter it to suit your lyrics. This does work, and some very good music has been written this way. The obvious danger is that you're flirting with copyright infringement if you don't actually change the melody. It takes very little copying to be in violation of the law and to raise the ethical question of stealing someone else's creative output. Therefore, the only way to appropriately use this method is to think of the existing melody as a pattern against which you write a new melody with different timing, different note progressions, and different note values.

Throughout the history of modern popular music (from the early part of this century through today) you'll find that certain chord progressions are repeated in tune after tune. That is because the general public feels comfortable with them. Just because they've been used over and over doesn't mean they shouldn't be used again. Standard progressions, such as I VI II V7 (in the key of C this translates to Cmaj Am7 Dm7 G7), or blues progressions, such as I7 IV7 V7, are found in tune after tune. They're probably in some of those ten favorite songs you're studying, since both modern rock and country have their base roots in blues. Weaker chord changes, such as Cmaj to B♭maj in the key of C, or Am to Em in the key of C, should be used sparingly for contrast or emphasis. The use of each chord progression depends on the sound that you're trying to create.

After you've laid down the basic chord progression that you're going to use for a song, go back and look at each tonality. It isn't enough to sell a tune with a I IV V progression if you can find a better chord to improve the tune or make it sound unique. Finding the right chord for the tone of the tune is what will make the song work. There are five basic types of chord qualities you can use to add flavor to your music: major chords, minor chords, dominant chords, diminished chords, and half diminished chords. Each type has its own unique feeling, and that feeling changes from key to key. There are many choices to make when combining chords in your song. You can, for example, use a chord that is outside the key of the main body of the song, if you employ it as a passing tool, to connect one section to another. The rules for the use of chords will really depend upon your ear and your musical taste.

In any event, try not to go overboard and use too many chord changes just for the sake of complexity or to demonstrate your expertise to other musicians. If you sell the tune and it becomes popular, it really doesn't matter if other musicians grouse about your skill. You have the money and reputation for having sold the tune; they don't.

PUTTING IT TOGETHER AND ARRANGING IT

After you've gotten the song written—you have words, melody, and chords—stand back and look at the whole product. Does the music really fit the words? Have you said what you wanted to say so that it's both understandable and "catchy"? Is it all one tune, or have you really written parts of two or three different tunes that should be taken apart and separately developed? This is one of the more common mistakes of amateur songwriters. Regardless of any technical flaws, does the tune stand by itself as an individual piece of music, at least on an emotional level?

Another composing error is falling in love with what you've written and being unwilling or creatively unable to reappraise the work and rewrite it. It isn't always easy to become objective about your own creative output; however, everyone else will be incredibly objective and maybe even negatively subjective. So it's best to be as critical as possible with your work before subjecting it to outside analysis.

Another way to err is to fall in love with what you're saying—your message to the world—and to disregard the actual performance value of the tune. Will it sell in East Peoria, Illinois? Will people your age in the cities, on the farms, in the suburbs, and in factory towns accept what you've written? These questions are not easy to answer. What you must do is determine if your song has what it takes to sell to a live audience today. By the way, the opinions of your friends are essentially meaningless. The opinions of a club audience are almost as meaningless, unless someone asks for "that tune you did last night." If they remember the hook, you're on the right track.

An essential part of preparing a tune for performance is arranging it: determining the style and instrumentation that will support the music and suit your needs. Before you plan an arrangement, determine if you've written a song for your group to play, or a tune that can be sold to other artists. Take into consideration if you want to showcase the song, or the group doing the song. Who else could do the tune? Could it be done in a different style altogether, such as rock instead of country or reggae instead of rock? Could it be done with an entirely different tempo?

What about the long-term crossover potential of the tune? Could it be performed by Steve Lawrence on "The Tonight Show"? Could it be made into elevator music? Songs that can cross over and fit into a number of different molds have a greater potential for long-range financial return than one-category songs. On the other hand, songs that will showcase a group and put them into the national spotlight have an obvious value of their own.

As you arrange your tune keep your purpose in mind. If you're using the music to push your group, then the arrangement of your original tune can be handled in the same way as any other tune you put into your repertoire. You can use the techniques that create your band's special sound. If you are trying to sell the song to another artist, decide if you're after a current dance hit position or want the tune to be a "standard." Big moneymaking, short-life-span dance tunes should be arranged with the type of production that will get people up to dance. This kind of production fluctuates with the times, so don't use outmoded sounds or rhythm tracks.

If you think you've written a standard, ask yourself these questions: Does the melody stand alone with just a vocal and piano or guitar? Do the words make sense and have universal appeal? Does the range of the melody stay within or around an octave to an octave-and-a-half? If you do have a standard on your hands, or an MOR crossover tune, then the production of the tune can be very, very simple. Start by laying down just a solo instrument and a voice. Then add complementary instruments and harmonies to provide a carpet of sound behind the lyrics. Normally, the vocals take center stage in a standard, and the lyrics exude a heartwarming appeal.

It is always good to have someone else help you arrange your original song so that it doesn't become overly ingrown. This person can be another band member, a studio producer, or a musical collaborator. Always copyright your tunes before presenting them to other musicians or people in the music business. Copyrighting isn't as difficult or expensive as you might imagine, and it can make all the difference in the world if you happen to write a platinum-selling song.

COPYRIGHTS

Under current copyright law a song is considered copyrighted as soon as it's put into tangible, final form, that is, written down on paper or recorded on tape. The hassle comes with establishing proof of authorship and date of origin. There are various agencies that will "protect" your material for a small fee, but that protection is no more binding in court than sending a copy of the song to yourself by registered mail and keeping the receipt and sealed envelope in a safe place. To establish absolute copyright proof you must register the material with the Library of Congress. This can be done in written or tape form. Melody and words are necessary for the complete song, but you can copyright separately your lyrics or your instrumental tune. Chords are not necessary unless they are unique to the song. However, most songwriters do want their particular chord progressions protected if they've put a lot of work into them and used unusual voicings.

It costs ten dollars to copyright one or a collection of songs. For prolific writers, it's best to send a collection ("Songs by John C. Doe") for one ten-dollar charge. You must use Form PA. (See sample on next page.) You may not use a photocopied form from the local library. To get as many forms as you need, call (202) 287-9100 at any time, and leave a recorded message asking for Form PA and giving your address. Or write to: Copyright Office, Library of Congress, Washington, DC 20559.

To secure a copyright, send a check or money order for ten dollars and the complete song or collection of songs either charted out or on tape, all at the same time. You will receive complete instructions with the forms. Be aware that if your song is recorded for airplay, published, or bought by a major name or label, they will have to recopyright the tune. If you have not already established proof of copyright, you may have to take someone to court to protect your rights. It is not possible to sell your copyright. Once you have established authorship with the Library of Congress, you can never have it taken away (unless someone else sent the tune in first). Regardless of any contract that you may sign in the future, your authorship cannot be removed from the face of that tune. No other agency or service can give you such complete protection.

Sample Copyright Form PA

FORM PA
UNITED STATES COPYRIGHT OFFICE

REGISTRATION NUMBER

PA	PAU

EFFECTIVE DATE OF REGISTRATION

Month	Day	Year

DO NOT WRITE ABOVE THIS LINE. IF YOU NEED MORE SPACE, USE A SEPARATE CONTINUATION SHEET.

1 TITLE OF THIS WORK ▼

PREVIOUS OR ALTERNATIVE TITLES ▼

NATURE OF THIS WORK ▼ See instructions

2

a NAME OF AUTHOR ▼

DATES OF BIRTH AND DEATH
Year Born ▼   Year Died ▼

Was this contribution to the work a "work made for hire"?
☐ Yes
☐ No

AUTHOR'S NATIONALITY OR DOMICILE
Name of Country
OR { Citizen of ▶
Domiciled in ▶

WAS THIS AUTHOR'S CONTRIBUTION TO THE WORK
Anonymous? ☐ Yes ☐ No
Pseudonymous? ☐ Yes ☐ No

If the answer to either of these questions is "Yes," see detailed instructions.

NATURE OF AUTHORSHIP   Briefly describe nature of the material created by this author in which copyright is claimed. ▼

NOTE

Under the law, the "author" of a "work made for hire" is generally the employer, not the employee (see instructions). For any part of this work that was "made for hire" check "Yes" in the space provided, give the employer (or other person for whom the work was prepared) as "Author" of that part, and leave the space for dates of birth and death blank.

b NAME OF AUTHOR ▼

DATES OF BIRTH AND DEATH
Year Born ▼   Year Died ▼

Was this contribution to the work a "work made for hire"?
☐ Yes
☐ No

AUTHOR'S NATIONALITY OR DOMICILE
Name of country
OR { Citizen of ▶
Domiciled in ▶

WAS THIS AUTHOR'S CONTRIBUTION TO THE WORK
Anonymous? ☐ Yes ☐ No
Pseudonymous? ☐ Yes ☐ No

If the answer to either of these questions is "Yes," see detailed instructions.

NATURE OF AUTHORSHIP   Briefly describe nature of the material created by this author in which copyright is claimed. ▼

c NAME OF AUTHOR ▼

DATES OF BIRTH AND DEATH
Year Born ▼   Year Died ▼

Was this contribution to the work a "work made for hire"?
☐ Yes
☐ No

AUTHOR'S NATIONALITY OR DOMICILE
Name of Country
OR { Citizen of ▶
Domiciled in ▶

WAS THIS AUTHOR'S CONTRIBUTION TO THE WORK
Anonymous? ☐ Yes ☐ No
Pseudonymous? ☐ Yes ☐ No

If the answer to either of these questions is "Yes," see detailed instructions.

NATURE OF AUTHORSHIP   Briefly describe nature of the material created by this author in which copyright is claimed. ▼

3 YEAR IN WHICH CREATION OF THIS WORK WAS COMPLETED   This information must be given in all cases.   ◀ Year

DATE AND NATION OF FIRST PUBLICATION OF THIS PARTICULAR WORK
Complete this information ONLY if this work has been published.
Month ▶ _____ Day ▶ _____ Year ▶ _____   ◀ Nation

4 COPYRIGHT CLAIMANT(S) Name and address must be given even if the claimant is the same as the author given in space 2.▼

See instructions before completing this space.

TRANSFER If the claimant(s) named here in space 4 are different from the author(s) named in space 2, give a brief statement of how the claimant(s) obtained ownership of the copyright.▼

DO NOT WRITE HERE OFFICE USE ONLY

APPLICATION RECEIVED

ONE DEPOSIT RECEIVED

TWO DEPOSITS RECEIVED

REMITTANCE NUMBER AND DATE

MORE ON BACK ▶
• Complete all applicable spaces (numbers 5-9) on the reverse side of this page.
• See detailed instructions.
• Sign the form at line 8.

DO NOT WRITE HERE
Page 1 of _____ pages

DO NOT WRITE ABOVE THIS LINE. IF YOU NEED MORE SPACE, USE A SEPARATE CONTINUATION SHEET.

PREVIOUS REGISTRATION Has registration for this work, or for an earlier version of this work, already been made in the Copyright Office?

☐ **Yes** ☐ **No** If your answer is "Yes," why is another registration being sought? (Check appropriate box) ▼

☐ This is the first published edition of a work previously registered in unpublished form.

☐ This is the first application submitted by this author as copyright claimant.

☐ This is a changed version of the work, as shown by space 6 on this application.

If your answer is "Yes," give: **Previous Registration Number ▼**   **Year of Registration ▼**

5

DERIVATIVE WORK OR COMPILATION Complete both space 6a & 6b for a derivative work; complete only 6b for a compilation.

a. Preexisting Material Identify any preexisting work or works that this work is based on or incorporates. ▼

b. Material Added to This Work Give a brief, general statement of the material that has been added to this work and in which copyright is claimed. ▼

6

See instructions before completing this space.

DEPOSIT ACCOUNT If the registration fee is to be charged to a Deposit Account established in the Copyright Office, give name and number of Account.

Name ▼   **Account Number ▼**

7

CORRESPONDENCE Give name and address to which correspondence about this application should be sent.   Name/Address/Apt/City/State/Zip ▼

Area Code & Telephone Number ▶

Be sure to give your daytime phone ◀ number.

CERTIFICATION* I, the undersigned, hereby certify that I am the

Check only one ▼

☐ author

☐ other copyright claimant

☐ owner of exclusive right(s)

☐ authorized agent of_____
　　　Name of author or other copyright claimant, or owner of exclusive right(s) ▲

8

of the work identified in this application and that the statements made by me in this application are correct to the best of my knowledge.

Typed or printed name and date ▼ If this is a published work, this date must be the same as or later than the date of publication given in space 3.

_____ date ▶ _____

Handwritten signature (X) ▼

MAIL CERTIFI-CATE TO

Name ▼

Number/Street/Apartment Number ▼

Certificate will be mailed in window envelope

City/State/ZIP ▼

Have you:
• Completed all necessary spaces?
• Signed your application in space 8?
• Enclosed check or money order for $10 payable to *Register of Copyrights?*
• Enclosed your deposit material with the application and fee?

MAIL TO: Register of Copyrights. Library of Congress, Washington, D.C. 20559

9

Learning Songs

WHEN YOU'RE learning tunes, it's important to stick to a format. Having a format means keeping all the songs in your repertoire along the same basic groove. This is especially important when presenting original material in showcases or on a recording. People like to be able to label what they hear, so they know how to enjoy it. A good illustration of what is really meant today by the word "variety" is the club owner's line: "We like both kinds of music here—country and western." The point is not to make all your tunes sound the same; just make sure they're all within the same general classification.

Deciding on a format isn't as difficult as it sounds. Most musicians know if they want to play country, rock, heavy metal, jazz, or top 40, and will team up with other players who want to do the same stuff. A problem will normally arise only when original music is involved, because writers do not necessarily produce one style of music exclusively. A top 40 guitarist may find that he's written what is unquestionably a country song, along with a couple of top 40 tunes and two undeniably heavy metal pieces. Don't mix them up to show off your versatility. Take the stuff that isn't part of your basic format and demo it to sell to someone else. Keep only the music that fits your format in the repertoire.

Realizing that what you've written is not necessarily what you play can be a real crisis for a new writer, and the first thing you'll probably do is deny that the tunes are outside the format. Hopefully, you'll realize this or be shown the light before any real damage is done, and you'll be able to keep your particular groove intact so that the audience doesn't get confused. An audience that can't easily classify your music will turn off to you, no matter how good you are and no matter how wonderful or original your material is. People like to know what's coming up next. Surprises are for movies.

STEPS TO LEARNING MUSIC

If you know how to play your axe, you know how to learn music, right? Wrong. Unfortunately, getting the whole group to learn the same song on the same time schedule isn't always that easy. New groups of players who don't have years of experience and tons of songs to fall back on can waste a lot of time—months—in garages and rehearsal halls putting together thirty workable tunes. Forget that. Start with a formula for learning music and keep to it.

First, get a recording of the song. (If it's an original, make a simple instrument and voice recording.) Give everyone a copy of the tape. Have everyone go home and learn their parts—chords, melody, and words. If it is a particularly difficult tune to take off the recording, find the sheet music and give everyone a copy. When you hand out the tapes or sheets, set the time for a later rehearsal so everyone knows when they have to have their parts down. Start off by having everyone learn a "record copy" version of the song, that is, lick for lick off the record. This sells best in top 40 rooms. It is also the best way to learn the tune initially and to get used to taking music off a record. If you can't figure out what chords are being played by listening to them on a tape, work on it until you can. It is essential to your career as a musician that you develop your ears. All this is done with practice, something that many musicians think they left behind in school. Practice is getting your individual chops up; rehearsal is putting a song together with a band. If the members of the band each practice sufficiently, rehearsal time can be effective and kept reasonably short.

While doing straight record copy is the most recognizable way to arrange a song, it is also the least artistic. Someone else has done all the work for you. When your group feels that it wants to develop its own sound, work with the arrangement of the tunes to make them fit the sound of your band.

Approach original tunes in a similar, same-technique-all-the-time way. Hand out the tape to be learned, then let the band members learn or develop their parts in practice. Bring all the ideas together for a rehearsal. If you want to have more specific control over your creation or if you're building a backup group to showcase your writing, pass out the tapes with specific instructions on what part is to be added by what player, and how and when the part is to be played. Have your group go home and practice what you've given them. If you're not musically up to giving specific instructions, you may have to collaborate with someone who is, or hire a concert master. Either way, unless you have a great deal of time to waste or a long-standing band with a well-developed sound, don't try to learn music in a clump session. Everyone will still have to go home to practice their parts. If you have a player with a lazy streak, and you let him get away with murder the first time, he probably won't bother to learn his part until the next rehearsal. Develop a formula for learning new tunes, both original and cover, and stick with it.

If you've got a great cover tune but it just doesn't work for your group, stop doing it, even if it's still on the radio. If you don't pull it off well, it will become an embarrassment. The tricky part of this is that at first you may not be aware the song isn't working; you don't feel embarrassed at all, but your audience does. Avoid this by making doubly sure you do the song well, or don't do it at all.

When you're developing your formula for learning new tunes, be aware of the possible need for noninstrumental rehearsals to get all the vocal parts down tight. The vocals and rhythm section are the two most important elements of a live performance and may require separate rehearsal time. Rhythm section rehearsals (bass, drums, and percussion) may be the key to making your band more saleable than the next one. Again, make sure everyone has practiced their parts before the rehearsal and is ready to work on getting tight as a unit. For vocal rehearsals, if possible, try to hand out harmony parts ahead of time. If this isn't possible, stage two rehearsals, one to find all the parts and one to put them together after everyone has gone home and practiced. You often hear about groups who spend weeks, months, even years rehearsing before going out to try their luck. This is called stalling and has no place in the reality of the music business. Get your efficient formula down and get on with it.

ARRANGING COVER TUNES

In any kind of tune, original or cover, the same arrangement techniques can apply. Determine the tradition of the cover tune. How has it been played in the past? Is there any one arrangement that is absolutely necessary? Remember that to change an old, familiar tune will anger someone in your audience. When you perform an original tune onstage or on vinyl, you'll be establishing the tradition of that tune for others to follow and they will have to agonize over the same decision.

Arrangements of songs can be reworked or personalized by changing the beat, shifting the tempo, adding repeats and stops, setting up key modulations, changing harmonic voicings, making a solo tune into a boy/girl tune (and vice versa), or adding a repeating musical riff. You can probably think of other ways of altering tunes to fit your image and sound once you start playing around with a song. The more tunes you make "personal," the more your audience will identify and remember you.

3

THE
SHOW

Club groups seldom put on scripted shows; they play sets. But someday you may want to do more than play clubs. You have hopes, dreams, and aspirations. You'd better also have some knowledge of theatrical performance, advertising, and the technical requirements of staging a show.

Developing a Show

IF YOU'RE going to make the step from neighborhood or traveling club band to showcasing and beyond, you're going to need a show. A performer must have either a love of playing or a love of performing (a need to be onstage) to pull off a successful show. Audiences can sense disinterest or lack of enthusiasm. You have to maintain a sustained passion for your performance activity, whatever it is. You also need an insurmountable, irrepressible resistance to rejection. More than anything else, you should be aware that when you are onstage, you aren't just playing music; you're delivering entertainment. People play music by turning on a stereo. People go out to watch a show. It's the old "shave and shower" principle: a person comes home from working a full day, showers, changes clothes, gets into the car, drives to your show, puts down money for drinks, and sits back to be entertained. It's your job to distract him from his everyday thoughts and problems, make him feel happy, and send him home revived and refreshed. And if you haven't figured out yet that you have to give more to your audience than you can expect to get back from them, you're not ready to call yourself a pro.

To give a professional performance, you have to work out a show. To put on a show, you have to know what your multiple functions are onstage. You have to present a specific image through clothing, attitude, and posture. You have to be aware of acting and performing techniques, and you have to follow a script. This is a craft, after all, and it takes time, knowledge, practice, and flexibility.

ONSTAGE FUNCTIONS

Each member of a band usually has a function onstage in addition to performing. A group has to have a stage leader or conductor, if not an actual leader. It needs a front, an announcer, and one or two featured performers to give the audience a change from time to time. Each one of these functions should be handled by a different person, if possible. The announcer should be the member with the best "radio" voice, and preferably should not be the lead singer or stage leader. It's his function to announce the band when they come onstage, introduce the band members at the end of the show, and introduce any specialty number or featured performance. If you are a solo artist, your announcer can also play the part of sidekick to create the kind of onstage relationship that audiences enjoy so much.

The stage leader is the person who conducts the band onstage. Preferably, this person should not be the front. The stage leader begins and ends the tunes by cue. He also gives the cue to extend or cut short any tune, depending on the audience's reaction.

The front should be the performer who is most dynamic, preferably the lead singer, but definitely the person with the most charisma—the one who can attract the attention of everyone in the audience. The image that the front presents will be perceived by the audience as the image of the entire band, so his personality must come across through his instrument and the microphone. Use whatever gimmicks are necessary to accentuate the front and his image, because he must develop the persona of the band. This is essential and should not be left to chance. If you are a solo artist, be sure that you can control the stage and do not lose the audience's attention to any of your support personnel.

The featured performer (other than the lead singer) should have the ability to sing a few songs. Showcasing this player in a single tune or segment of a tune will provide a break in the show and add audience appeal. This kind of feature develops a mystique around the featured performer, thereby adding to the mystique and appeal of the band as a whole. Creating a mystique around a band is vitally important for a group that wants to progress, because the audience wants to feel "privileged" to know you. Does that sound corny? Corn sells. This is show biz.

ONSTAGE PLACEMENT

If you have a specific setup during rehearsals that you're accustomed to, use that setup onstage. Spread out enough to be comfortable, but don't spread out to fill the stage if it results in being too far away from each other. Stay tight enough to maintain the feeling of a unit. If you're not using a rehearsal hall or large room to rehearse in and have no set placement, use a standard band setup. Put the drums in the rear, on a riser if possible, but not so far back that the player is out of communication with the stage leader and bass player. Bass and backup instruments or vocalists should be slightly forward of the drums, well within sight of the audience and the stage leader, positioned on either side of the drummer but not directly in front of him. The front should be out front—way out front. He has to draw the attention of everyone who looks at the stage. If your stage is in a bar or club that has little space for spreading out or moving forward, then, of course, you'll have to make your setup more compact. (This will almost always be true of local bars.) Keep the positions as close as possible to what you've previously worked out.

CLOTHING

It is important to be aware of the fact that although you are going to work every night, you are not going to a job; you are putting on a show. Thus you should appear in costume. Your band should be uniformed. The words "costume" and "uniforms" do not mean theatrical outfits of different eras or marching-band getups. They refer to clothes that project a specific image in keeping with the identity of the band as a whole—an image that sets the band members, as a group and individually, apart from the members of the audience.

Good general rules for costuming your band might include keeping a universal article of clothing (shirts or pants, for example) a matching color, but of different styles. Make another clothing item match in style but be different colors. Use matching accessories if everyone is in different styles and colors, or have everyone wear the same color and use different accessories to individualize the members. Have your front use accessories or bright colors to draw people's attention. The front does not have to adhere to the rest of the band's styles or colors, but he must be visually linked with the other members in some way. Therefore, if all the musicians in your band are wearing conservative suits and ties, the front should be dressed in a similar mode but more colorfully or less conservatively, or maybe even formally. If your band is wearing matching jeans and T-shirts, your front can dress in jeans and a T-shirt, too; he should wear a hat or a bandanna, though, or something that accentuates his special role.

The various accessories that can be used to individualize band members include: loose ties, bandannas, wide belt buckles, hats, sweatbands on wrists (especially good for the drummer), boots, vests, and fashion jackets. The object is to have each band member appear as a dynamic performer in his own right while maintaining a coherent image for the band as a whole and having the front be the most visually striking person onstage.

All of this—knowing your function, keeping to a familiar setup, having a good visual image—is more important than many bands like to think. Picture the last time you saw your favorite group: were they set up the same way as the time before? When you think back to the Beatles, for example, you have no problem visualizing them onstage, because they always set up the same way. And they always dressed like one band, rather than a bunch of guys who got onstage together accidentally. Having a distinctive style for your group gives the audience one more handle for remembering you. Since you are probably competing with two or three hundred groups in your immediate area you have to use every method available to leave an impression on the people who see you perform.

PERFORMANCE

This is what it's all about: performing your songs. Except that performing your songs means more than just playing music—it means performing, which is a theatrical concept. When you put on a show for an audience you are elevating your musical presentation from the rehearsal or local bar stage up to the level of show business or theatrical entertainment. Now you have a responsibility to your audience, so you must know who they are, what they expect, and how to deliver the goods.

Identify Your Audience. What people do you, individually, want to impress when you get onstage: girls, men, other musicians, the general public? Whom do you, as a band, want to impress? Are they the same targets that you as an individual have? Can the differences be reconciled? What age group does your music really appeal to? Does your visual image match the audience you're playing to? It is important to have a target audience. It is also important to aim for a broad-based audience so that you don't end up with only a cult following.

Define Your Objectives. Clarifying your onstage goals may be the most important offstage thing you can do. Most groups have only vague objectives when they climb up on a club stage. They may have notions of keeping the gig or simply making some money. Maybe they're thinking they can "go somewhere" if they get good enough.

Your objectives each time you go onstage to perform your music should be the following:

▶ to entertain the audience enough that they stay for your entire performance

▶ to make the show and the group memorable enough that people will remember the band's name the next day

▶ to stimulate the audience enough that they would want to see the same show again

▶ to impress the owner/operator enough so that you are asked back

▶ to exercise and develop your skills as a performer for future appearances in order to accomplish all of the above

▶ finally, to play your music

Stage Attitude. Carry yourself as if you own the stage and belong on it by divine right. It should be the normal and expected state of affairs for you to be performing onstage and for people to be listening and appreciating. To develop this kind of posture, you have to display complete self control and stage control. Avoid displaying even a hint of embarrassment or insecurity about your music, your performance, or your onstage presence. If you make a mistake, no one in the audience should be able to identify it as something that wasn't planned. Develop an intensity throughout the show, especially between tunes. Feel removed from your audience without being aloof or disinterested. Don't act intrinsically superior to the audience; rather, be unabashed about being the center of attention. Have fun onstage so that your audience has fun watching you. Use your stage posture to develop an extremely high energy flow that you transmit to the audience. It must be stimulating to be a part of your show by being in the audience.

A point to remember: the audience must become part of the performance. That is the responsibility of the front—to capture the audience's attention and allegiance so that they feel as though they are part of what is happening in the room. They will stay for the entire performance because they are involved in it. They will remember the band because they are proud of their affiliation with it. They will return night after night because of the lift they get. The operator will want to bring the band back again and again because it does good business for him. And guess what? You get to play your tunes, too.

Etiquette. Etiquette is tactfulness. Tactfulness is polite omission. In other words, you need to know what not to say and, most important, when not to say it. For example, imagine you're onstage doing a tune, and the drummer loses a beat. Don't turn around and yell at him while the song is being played. Don't ask him what the hell he thinks he's doing as soon as the song ends. Don't throw nasty looks at him for the rest of the show. Don't make a belittling remark to the audience or off-mike about his lack of ability, his stupid habits, or the fact that he screwed up the whole tune. Go on as if nothing happened.

When he does the same thing on the next three tunes and you are as furious as you can possibly get, don't collar him during the break and try to break his neck. Don't take him out to the parking lot and scream bloody murder. Don't huddle with the other band members and make plans to dismember him. Don't sit down with friends, bar people, the operator, or customers and complain about your lousy drummer and how you're going to cut his throat, and don't say, "The band usually sounds so much better than this, honest." Don't do any of these things; they're poor etiquette. They're also unprofessional and messy.

The basic rules of etiquette are: avoid getting involved in any confrontation during times of anger or when you're under the influence of your performance "high." Never display negativity during the course of a gig—from the time you leave for the club to the point when you go home. Save angry remarks and accusations for the next morning, when you have cooled down enough to think clearly and act effectively. Confrontations should never be witnessed by an audience, and that includes friends, bar personnel, boyfriends, and girlfriends. Avoid being unpleasant anywhere in the performance arena. (Notable exceptions, of course, are scripted punk or hard rock shows, in which surliness is an expected part of the act.) If for some reason a discussion has to come down during a break in order to save the next set, do whatever is necessary to get yourself calm and detached from the problem before walking quietly with the transgressor to a really private area; then quietly and calmly work out the problem.

"Etiquette" sounds like an elaborate way to describe a common-sense attitude that all performers should have. Ignoring it, however, is a mistake that is too commonly made. Remember that everything you do or say while you are in a club, a showcase room, or a concert hall will be watched and noted. Etiquette on the gig is a necessary indication of professionalism to your audience, the operator, your colleagues, and any industry observers that may be there to catch your show. Even more, a lack of etiquette indicates that you are an amateur and, as such, can be dismissed from serious consideration.

Characterization. You will need to develop good theatrical skills to sustain your onstage persona. First, decide who or what your performance character is. Are you a raging drummer? Are you a quiet, straightfaced bass player? Do you see yourself as the personification of sex, or as a happy-go-lucky party boy? Make faces in a mirror until you find the one that best shows the way you feel about the person you are onstage. Examine your offstage personality and determine what part of it would be most appealing onstage. Work on exaggerating that part of your personal makeup. Become comfortable with your onstage persona by playacting. Playacting will help you to overcome any embarrassment you might have about creating a stage character. Do exercises or aerobics with the other band members to help you learn how to move your body in specific, easy-flowing ways that blend well with the other people onstage. This will also help you to overcome any sense of silliness or embarrassment you might experience in front of the other musicians.

Acting and Performing Skills. When you know who you are onstage, you must be able to communicate that personality to the audience. In a musical presentation, that communication is accomplished through the lyrics and emotion of the songs performed, as well as through your personal charisma and acting skills. Musicians are often opposed to the idea of acting classes, believing (no doubt) that acting means being phony. On the contrary, acting is a controlled, rehearsed way of communicating your thoughts and emotions. After performing a tune hundreds of times, it is obviously no longer fresh for you. Unless you have developed the skills necessary to bring a tune to life every time you perform it, it will become stale for you and for your audience. Eventually, the tune will become a liability rather than an asset. Actors in long-running plays are called upon to say the same lines in the same way thousands of times, and make each audience feel that they have been given the best performance. You must achieve the same level of professionalism for your musical show if you intend to have a long-term career in the public eye. Furthermore, the verbal interludes between songs have to be spoken in the ninety-fifth show with the same enthusiasm and apparent inspiration as they were in the first show. This requires a mastery of acting skills that you can acquire through college classes, band workshops, or intensive on-the-job self-training.

Onstage Techniques. Here are just a few general ideas you can use to communicate your onstage character:

▶ If you're the front, play at the edge of the stage. Look at the audience, not at your instrument or the other band members. Make eye-to-eye contact with someone in the audience and play directly to that person. If you habitually make faces or use distinct facial expressions, direct them specifically to someone. Remember to perform with total confidence. If you feel you're making a fool of yourself, you might as well go all the way and make it good.

▶ Demand the musicians' undivided attention by giving them your undivided attention. Pick out some fans in the audience and force your energy onto them; then take it back. It is said that the Rolling Stones insist that the first twenty rows of any show they give be filled with screaming fans, rather than with important industry people. They derive energy from their fans which spurs them on to a great performance.

▶ If you are a front, it is your job to be a visual focus. Picture yourself on television. Watch yourself in your mind's eye and be interesting. Performing is not like being an office clerk. If you're not exhausted at the end of the night, you're not putting out enough.

▶ If you aren't the front, keep in mind that it is your job to provide the power behind him. Perform more, play less. Communicate lyrics and emotions. Don't just play the tune. Act as if you are an SRO band, even if the room is empty. Play to every audience as if you were opening for a major act: you have to win over their audience, hold your own on their turf, and not get booed off the stage by their impatient fans. Almost all major acts have had to conquer that challenge at one point or another. Start learning to do it now.

▶ Feel yourself as part of a tight unit with the other band members. Pull energy from each other, reinforce it with your own, and send it out to the audience. Remember to accentuate your own onstage persona as well as the band's image.

▶ Picture yourself on "The Tonight Show," "Star Search," "Saturday Night Live," or in concert on HBO. Use your mind's eye to watch yourself as you perform, and live up to what you'd expect to see on camera.

SCRIPTS AND SET LISTS

Shows are delivered by script. You don't need one, but you won't hold anyone's attention if you turn around after every song to discuss what you're going to do next. People want to feel that you care enough to plan ahead.

Scripts can be as complex as knowing exactly what word and inflection comes next or as simple as a set list. Professionals who play concert halls use the complex, word-for-word, same-inflection-every-night type of script and apply their acting skills to make it seem spontaneous. That is your goal.

To start out, do make a set list. Decide which songs are going to have verbal introductions and what those introductions are going to be. Decide who is going to do the introduction; hopefully, it will be the announcer or singer of the tune. Give everyone a copy of the set list with current keys noted. Onstage is not the place to start searching your mind for what key you finally decided to do that next song in. Plan one or two story-type introductions to give the audience a little more of a personal connection to you or the group. Keep the stories short, down to one to three sentences. For example, "Chris wrote this tune for his wife on the night she said she'd marry him. Now they've got two little girls." This gives the audience a feeling of intimacy with you, which helps to establish that feeling of identification and allegiance you want. Also, it sets up the tune as something special and worthy of attention.

Group your tunes according to tempo and break the pace of the show with verbal remarks between groups of tunes. Remember, your audience wants to know what's going on and to be involved in the performance.

The following is an example of a script for a one-hour set. It is only an example; there can be hundreds of variations on this theme.

▶ Verbal introduction, from offstage if the gig is a showcase or beginning set.

▶ First song—short, uptempo, and powerful. Go into the song and out of it fast, with no long musical solos.

▶ Verbal introduction by the front: "Good evening and welcome to our show."

▶ Second song—equally uptempo, but not quite as intense as the first.

▶ Third song—uptempo.

▶ A short story—cute, but not too long—to draw the audience back into the performance.

▶ Fourth song—slower, possibly a ballad.

▶ Fifth song—moderately paced tune.

▶ Sixth song—moderate- or slow-paced tune.

▶ Tell a joke. Make a remark that's funny. Somehow get the audience to laugh. Keep this short and simple, but let the front show his stuff, verbally.

▶ Introduce a featured performer with a story about the person or the tune that's coming up. This should be specifically scripted and carried out with a flourish as if the front were expansively turning his stage over to someone else for a song. Communicate graciousness, rather than sarcasm, through the words of the announcer or the front.

▶ Seventh song—highlighted tune by featured performer.

▶ Eighth song—uptempo. Go into this tune without a verbal break after the seventh song.

▶ Ninth song—uptempo.

▶ Tenth song—uptempo.

▶ Eleventh song—uptempo.

▶ Twelfth song—uptempo.

There should be no verbal breaks or dead time between the seventh song and the twelfth or thirteenth song. This is the meat of the show.

▶ Thirteenth song—uptempo (optional).

▶ Verbal introduction of the last tune by the announcer.

▶ Last song—should be the most powerful tune of the show or set. Sometime during this tune, have the announcer introduce the individual band members. Each player takes a two-bar solo at their introduction if it is done during the tune, otherwise do the introductions before the tune starts or during an extended ending.

▶ If this is a set, have the announcer tell the audience that the band will be back in a few minutes. Do this during the last few bars of the final song. If this is a show, wait for the song to end. Then have the front tell the audience that they've been a great audience (whether they have been or not) and thank them: "You've been a great audience; thank you very much."

▶ Get off the stage. Leave the instruments. If you're playing a club, do your audience work. Do not sit with friends. Do not just disappear. Do not sit in a huddle with other band members. If this is a show, when you get off the stage, go out the door. Let your roadies break down the stage set or wait until you can change clothes and come back inconspicuously to break it down. If you are part of a three- or five-band night and have to move your stuff quickly, then move it and go backstage or out the door with the equipment. In any event, don't sit around with your friends. Try to maintain the mystique you've worked so hard to develop on that stage.

Basic Performance Dos and Don'ts

▶ Do sell yourself; sell the show; sell the band; sell the songs—in that order.

▶ Don't hold off-mike discussions between songs.

▶ Don't allow dead time.

▶ Don't tell inside jokes even with friends in the audience who understand them. Your friends are not the part of the audience that you're trying to win over.

▶ Don't talk to each other off-mike at all. Once onstage, everything is on-mike, so pay attention to what is being said.

▶ Don't let your energy run down.

▶ Don't let the audience put you off. Insist that they pay attention to you by focusing all your attention on them.

▶ Do act as if you've just won your first Grammy and deserve and expect admiration and adulation from your audience. Give them the performance a Grammy winner would give.

▶ Do have a good time, and show it.

▶ Don't get hung up with the musical aspect of the performance over the entertainment aspect.

▶ Don't cast aspersions on the club you're in, or on any other club or performer. This doesn't mean you can't tell jokes, but don't screw yourself up by badmouthing anyone.

▶ Do demand energy from your audience by giving them yours.

▶ Don't let anyone, or anything that anyone says, psych you out. Be arrogant if necessary. Deny yourself your insecurity while you're onstage. Just do it.

▶ Do act as if you already have the security of a record contract and the adulation of the industry.

▶ Do perform as if *Billboard* magazine is reviewing the show.

▶ Don't get crude or vulgar. Don't let the arrogance of being onstage shift to an insulting attitude toward your audience.

Advertising a Show

YOU KNOW why advertising is important. You have to tell people where you're playing so they'll come to see you perform. You have to keep your band's name in the public eye so people will remember it. You have to keep the industry aware of your existence and progress so it stays aware of you. And you have to collect favorable articles and reviews for your own promotional use.

To advertise effectively you must recognize the variety of media available to you: print, radio, television, and publicity stunts. Then you must plan an effective advertising campaign.

PRINT

The print medium encompasses local newspapers, trade magazines, specific organization publications (such as the ones that Elk lodges and church groups put out), posters, banners, flyers to be distributed in store fronts and on street corners, and postcards or announcements to be sent to people on your mailing lists, which should include both industry people and fans. Print is the easiest and least expensive form of advertising, because you can do most of the work yourself. Draw up what you want on a poster. You can get your poster typeset and copied at a local print shop. Then distribute the posters where they will have the most visibility, such as in shop windows and on community or school bulletin boards. Send a press release to your local newspaper. (These may also be sent to radio and TV stations and to magazines. A sample press release is shown on page 95.) Underneath the heading "For Immediate Release," write a straightforward announcement of who you are and where and when you're performing. Also supply the name and phone number of the person to contact for additional information. Write a short article about the band and submit it to your local paper, either as a paid advertisement or as a review. Get interviewed by a local paper. Get reviewed by a local trade magazine. Getting publicity in these local papers isn't as difficult as it sounds. Small papers are always on the lookout for local news. Have a member of your band or support group approach the editor with a story idea. The paper may send a reporter to write an article. More frequently they'll let you submit one yourself, then they'll rewrite and edit it as they see fit. Also, build a mailing list. Take the names and addresses (on a nightly basis) of the people in your audience who really like the band. Make another list of people you want to impress in the industry. Print up announcements or hand write postcards informing everyone on your two mailing lists of where you're playing, where you're going, and so on. Use the print media to keep your name in circulation.

RADIO

There is public radio as well as private college stations. Some public stations have local band shows, where you can get widespread exposure with a clean demo tape. Many other public stations have free "concert lines," where you can list your upcoming performances. Private stations—college stations—will play cuts from your demo tape or interview you before an important gig if it is on campus or in a student-frequented club. Get to know which stations appeal to the same people as your music does (these are not necessarily the stations that you listen to) and use them to reach a larger audience. Radio exposure shouldn't cost you a lot of money if you research all the different routes beforehand and plan an effective airplay/live performance campaign.

TELEVISION

There are several kinds of television stations: network, public, local, and cable. Cable stations can be local or national; so can public stations. Find out about the local stations in your area—cable, public, and local network annexes. TV ad time is very expensive, so try to get free exposure on a local talent show or by being interviewed on a local talk show. You can try to get one of the local stations to do a feature on the club you're playing in, with your band spotlighted. Do a free performance as part of a class project for one of the college stations in your area. Get on the news by being part of a fundraising event staged by a major or local charity. TV exposure is more for long-term public awareness than specific performance advertising, so any time you can get on the air, you should take full advantage of the opportunity, even if you don't have a gig coming up right away.

PUBLICITY STUNTS

Publicity stunts are tough in this cynical I've-seen-it-all age. Skywriting is still effective for an immediate message, but people won't remember something they saw for a few seconds last week. The most effective thing you can do with a publicity stunt these days is to coordinate it with a radio station or local TV station so that you have definite coverage of the stunt. Becoming connected with a charity organization can give you the opportunity to stage a publicity stunt that will get your band in the news, get the charity in the news, and benefit everyone.

THE ADVERTISING CAMPAIGN

After you've decided what media you're going to advertise through and how you're going to word your ad, you should design a complete campaign. Know how much money you have to spend on each type of ad and how many types you're going to use. Plan the entire campaign in advance so that you have enough lead time for each medium. Posters, articles, and announcements should appear one week before a showcase, three weeks to a month before a concert, and two weeks before a club gig. TV spots and publicity stunt coverage should appear about the same time as the print media, if it can be arranged, or in the midst of a long layoff period, to keep your name alive. Plan to use your radio spots one to three days before a gig and during the course of a long-running gig. For example, on a long-term club gig, buy spots on Thursday, Friday, or Saturday to advertise that you're "still packing the house" but there's "always room for one more—come early!" TV coverage and publicity stunts can also be effective ways to remind fans of a long-term engagement. Don't slough off and rely on your advertising to fill the show, though. If your performance isn't up to the level of your ad, you'll find that the crowds leaving can be more damaging than a never-filled room.

Remember to target your audience through the media they would probably listen to or read most often. Don't overspend the first time out. Make a note for future campaigns of where your advertising money did the most good the first time. Try to get the operator of the club to cover the advertising costs, or at least to split the cost with you. Don't forget that you are advertising not only your band, but also the room that you're playing in, so build up the club as much as possible. Their business is your business. Don't relinquish control of your advertising to anyone, however, even if they are splitting the costs with you. Follow up on everything personally so that you know the ads are getting done correctly and on time. In the ad include important or special items about the club, but accentuate the band.

One final word: try not to get overly ambitious on your first foray into the advertising world. Although most musicians send out flyers or announcements to their mailing-list fans, they usually don't do anything else to put their name in front of the public. When you do take the next step, be careful. Do as much research into costs and exposure in your area as possible and plan a campaign that gets the most mileage out of your money in as many different and effective markets as possible. Advertising doesn't end with the gig. It should be an ongoing, relentless pursuit to make your name so familiar to the public that they look for news about you. It's okay to get bad press once in awhile; bad press can be overcome later by good press. No press is no good. It's better that people say your band stinks than have people ask "Who is that band?" Getting your name known is a first step toward securing your future.

Sample Press Release

— For Immediate Release —

Night Flyer, a four-piece rhythm and blues band, will appear in concert at the Easton Showroom next Saturday night at 10:30 P.M.

Night Flyer has gained a great deal of popularity in the East Bay area over the past three years. They have a strong following among college students and young professionals, who enjoy the band's repertoire of Motown standards, top 40 R&B, and original R&B music. The Showroom expects to have a sellout crowd, according to spokesman Bob Sherman.

Sherman, who is one of the managers of the Easton Showroom, said, "Night Flyer has a tight, funky sound, and the individual players are excellent. We've had many requests for them to play the room. We've just been waiting for the scheduling to work out, and, fortunately, it finally did. I think you can look forward to a really dynamite show."

Night Flyer includes Dana Davis on electric piano and synthesizers, Steve Knight on lead guitar, Frank Smith on drums, and Linda Karmen on vocals. Karmen was named First Runner-up in the recent East Bay Vocalist Contest.

In addition to their upcoming concert in Easton, the group is booked for a six-week concert tour, which will take them across the southern part of the state. They have also just finished recording a new EP called "The Allnighter," which will be available at the time of the concert.

Tickets for Saturday's performance are on sale now at the Easton Showroom box office. The ticket price is $7.50. For additional information, call the theater at 764-1234.

Staging a Show

YOU'VE GOT your act down. You've got the gig advertised. Now you have to go onstage and make it all sound and look good. To do that, you'll need to be able to make use of all the equipment at your disposal. Unfortunately, many musicians know little about the devices and materials they use onstage.

KNOWING THE STAGE

First, let's define some common terms. "Upstage" means away from the audience. "Downstage," then, is toward the audience. "Stage right" is on your right-hand side as you face the audience. "Stage left," of course, is on your left as you face the audience. Very simple.

Permanent sound boards are always stage right, so when you set up on any stage or are creating a placement layout for the band, keep the person who controls the board in a stage right position. If you have a soundman who runs the board from the back of the room through a snake, this is not a crucial matter. If you run the board from onstage, though, it is.

On a large stage, where you have a choice, it is often best to put your drummer upstage, stage left. Since most club stages don't have the room for creative positioning, the drummer almost always ends up upstage, center, with amps and speaker cabinets boxing him in.

Regardless of the room—be it club, concert hall, or showcase auditorium—find out the dimensions of the stage ahead of time so that you can plan any necessary adjustments to your usual setup. Find out the height of the stage, the depth, and the width. Find out if there are any trapdoors, or curtained-off backstage areas. Determine in advance where the power is located and whether it is earth grounded.

Know in advance about curtains, permanent speakers, and monitors so you can plan your setup ahead of time and not have to stand around trying to decide what to do two hours before you play.

Knowing the stage also includes being aware of the acoustical properties of surfaces off the stage. There are two kinds of acoustical surfaces: absorptive and reflective. This is essential information if you want all that carefully rehearsed material to be heard by everyone, much less heard clearly and enjoyably. Thick curtains and padding on the walls are absorptive surfaces. Hardwood floors or walls and mirrors or windows are reflective.

After you know how the room shapes up acoustically, you'll be able to do an effective sound check. If you have an absorptive stage, move the amps and monitors closer, so you can hear what you're playing and singing. If the stage is reflective, move everything back so that you don't get a distorted idea of what the audience is hearing, and so you don't blast out your ears. These are just general rules. Here, more specifically, are the different combinations of stage-to-audience acoustics that you must be aware of to set your levels properly.

▶ *An absorptive stage and a reflective audience:* Set sound levels from the back of the hall or room. Put your monitors right on top of you and put everything—all instruments and voices—through the monitors.

▶ *A reflective stage and an absorptive audience:* Do your sound check from the stage. You can add absorptive materials (such as rugs or curtains) onstage to tailor the sound.

▶ *An absorptive stage and an absorptive audience:* Set your sound levels from the back of the hall. The stage level may be intolerable for some performers, so adjust the monitors after the level of the room is set.

▶ *A reflective stage and a reflective audience:* Set the sound levels from the stage, at minimal. This kind of room needs little amplification since the sound will carry more than you think it will.

The ideal situation is to play in a "tuned room," that is, one that has wall paneling from the stage to the back of the room alternating absorptive and reflective surfaces. This kind of room is larger in width and height at the stage, tapering down toward the back of the audience. Opera halls, major auditoriums, and pre-microphone auditoriums are built this way.

There are two types of sound that may cause confusion during a sound check or performance. These are transient sound and ambient sound. Ambient sound is sound filling the room from the stage. Transient sound is sound bouncing off walls and coming back toward the stage, like an echo effect. Listening to transient sound—which is a delayed version of what you originally played—could throw off your entire performance. After you've done your sound check from the appropriate location for your type of room, listen to your monitors, not to the house, while you perform.

Always use monitors. They're not just crutches to make sure that you don't sing off key; they let you know how the sound is coming down onstage. The guys who tell you that they never used a monitor when they performed, back in their college or big band days, are talking about presophisticated-electronics performances, when monitors were not part of the setup. Today they are essential—unless you do an unamplified solo accordion act.

Don't position your speakers so that you are hearing them full force onstage. Even low volumes of intense or prolonged electronic sound can do damage to your hearing at close range. This brings us to the topic of sound reinforcement equipment.

SOUND REINFORCEMENT

The purpose of sound reinforcement is to deliver a clear, undistorted, amplified signal of the original source. This means that clarity without loudness is infinitely more effective than loudness without clarity. Your sound reinforcement (SR) equipment list should include microphones; a mixing board; effects or a crossover network to divide the frequencies into treble, midrange, and bass; amplifiers to evenly spread the sound; and a speaker system to transduce the audio signal back into the airwaves.

Okay, first set up the stage. Then wire all the instruments and mikes. Set up the snake, if applicable. A snake is an extension of the cables from the stage to the mixing board at another location. Mikes and instrument direct lines are plugged into a junction box called a "stage box." The snake extends from the stage box. Male connectors at the other end of the snake will be attached to female connectors on the mixing board. These types of connectors are called Cannon or XLR connectors. Three-quarter inch sockets are used to connect the stage amplifiers and monitor system to the mixing board. If you don't have a soundman to run the board from the back of the room, all of this is academic.

You know how to use a microphone. Hopefully, you know how to use your own amplifier and speaker system. The tricky part of the sound setup is at the mixing board, where every player and vocalist has an opinion—most of them wrong—about their personal EQing and volume.

The mixing board has five basic functions: separation of instrument and vocal sound, individual volume control of each channel used for a microphone or instrument, equalization, effects application, and placement (panning) of the sound between multiple speakers. You will have to adjust the EQ, the volume, the panning, and the effects.

Equalization. Individually adjust the EQ levels of each microphone or instrument in the following order: dominant instruments, recessive instruments, and vocals. (See chart on page 102.)

Dominant instruments are drums, percussion, brass or horns (but not woodwinds), pianos (electric and acoustic), and electric guitars.

Recessive instruments are synthesizers, lap steel guitars, acoustic guitars or stand-up bass, light percussion instruments (tambourine, triangle, maracas, claves), and woodwinds.

Vocals include all vocals—lead, backup, harmony, and verbal (non-singing).

EQing drums is the most important and most time-consuming process because drums are a multiple instrument. If you are miking the drums, you'll need at least two mikes—one for the kick drum and one for the snare. Don't mike cymbals unless you are playing in a two thousand-plus-capacity arena. Cymbals will be picked up by the open microphone.

Start with the bass drum. Set the mid and high (treble) ranges on neutral and adjust only the low (bass) range. Listen for the optimum projection with the least amount of reverberation or extraneous (ringing) sound. For the snare drum or tom-toms, set the high range on flat. Set the low range again for the optimum projection with the least amount of extraneous sound. Use the midrange to color or sweeten, lessening or strengthening the attack of the drum stroke. Always set the midrange past center to the right. Percussion instruments should be set, if miked separately, using the same process as for a snare or tom-tom.

Brass or other horns, not including woodwinds, use all three ranges for EQ. Set the bass range on +2 or +3 to the right of center. Set the midrange at +2 to +5 to the right of center. Set the treble range at +1 to +3 to the right of center. The only real exception to these settings is a trumpet. On a trumpet, set the treble range at −1 to −3 to the left of center.

An acoustical piano should be set up with two mikes, if possible. Use identical mikes. Put one on the upper part of the harp, halfway between middle C and the upper end of the harp. Put the other halfway between middle C and the lower end of the harp. Make sure that the mikes face the back of the piano. If you only have one mike to use on a grand piano, place it three quarters of the way up the harp from the right end of the piano, facing the rear. Always put the mike or mikes on a folded napkin or a thin towel if they're not already mounted on boom stands. With an electric piano, of course, no mikes are necessary as the piano has a direct line connection. For both types of pianos the EQ settings should all be set to the middle and then adjusted. Adjust the bass range to between +4 and +6. Midrange should be $+6$ to $+9$. Treble should be set between $+2$ and $+4$. You may find that you have to readjust these settings slightly, but try to stay within one number, plus or minus, of the basic settings.

An electric guitar gains its characteristic sound from the amp and from the effects that the guitar runs through, so unless you are in a recording studio and can add effects at the board, don't run your guitar in a direct line connection to the mixing board. To get a "concert mix"—that is, have everything running through the mixing board, including the guitar—hang a mike or place a mike on a stand in front of the amp and run the mike through the board.

EQ the guitar mike with the bass on $+2$, the mids on $+3$ to $+4\frac{1}{2}$ to the right of center, and the treble $+1$ to $+3\frac{1}{2}$ to the right of center. The amp should be turned up to full gain with the volume set by the master control on the board. This way, the amp can work at its full potential.

Recessive instruments should be EQed next. A lap steel guitar uses a direct line connection from the snake to the mixing board, or directly to the mixing board. EQ the lap steel using the same process as for the piano, but set the treble on -2 instead of $+2$.

A standup bass fiddle is either picked up with a mike on a stand or with an electronic pickup that attaches to the instrument. A bass guitar uses a direct line connection, but requires a "direct box," which is a passive device that connects the bass to the bass amp and sends a signal to the mixing board by way of the snake or a direct-line connection from the box. Set the bass range at $+6$, the mids at $+4$, and the treble at $+2$ for all types of bass instruments (including keyboard bass).

Light percussion instruments are either picked up by vocal mikes or miked separately. They should be set optimum flat (all three flat) except for a triangle, for which the treble should be set at $+3$ to give the optimum ringing.

Woodwinds are miked through vocal mikes and are set at $+2$ treble, mids at $+3$, and bass range at $+1$ to $+2$.

EQ the vocals last. Every singer has a particular style all his own,

Sample Mixing Board EQ Settings

Instruments	EQ Controls		
	High	Mid	Low
Brass, Saxophone	+1/+3	+2/+5	+2/+3
Trumpet	−1/−3	+2/+5	+2/+3
Acoustic & Electric Piano	+2/+4	+6/+9	+4/+6
Electric Guitar	+1/+3½	+3/+4½	+2
Lap Steel Guitar	−2	+6/+9	+4/+6
Basses	+2	+4	+6
Light Percussion	flat	flat	flat
Woodwinds	+2	+3	+1/+2

which may vary from the quieter songs to the more raucous ones. Set your EQ using the most vocally dynamic song in the repertoire. Start with all levels flat (set on center). Work with the treble and mid range at the same time. Bring them into the plus side of the settings very slowly, pushing as far as you can until you hear a hum or howling (feedback). Then turn them both down until you lose the feedback. Now set the bass range from +2 to +4, going as high within that range as possible without feeding back. Set the backup vocals in the same way as the lead vocals, although it isn't necessary to use the most dynamic song you have. Set the output controls (faders) on the mixing board so that the backup vocal mikes are one-third less than the lead vocal mike.

Other Adjustments. Volume should be adjusted according to the acoustical surfaces of the stage and hall you're playing in. Remember the absorptive and reflective surfaces. Keep in mind that if you are doing a sound check in an empty room, you will have to increase the master volume level later, when the room fills up with people. People are absorptive surfaces, too. Metal robots, on the other hand, are reflective.

In general, volumes should be set so that the vocals are out front, the lead instruments are just behind the vocals, and the rhythm section is present and driving, without being overpowering.

Panning is the placement of instruments and vocals in the five-point musical field. These points are center, near right, near left, far right, and far left. Panning refers to moving the entire sound unit to the different speakers to achieve a balance of sound at all points in the room. This is different from stereo, where you're splitting the sound by instrument or section into different speakers. Essentially, all you have to do is make sure you have the speakers set up so that the audience on the left side of the room can hear as well as the audience in the center or on the right side of the room. Set the volume at equal levels for all speakers.

Adjustments made to signal effects will be included in the EQ process. There are a variety of effects that you can run the vocals or instruments through before they come out in the final mix. Among them are echo units, reverb, delays, sibilance controls, limiters, and compressers. Many boards, of course, have a reverb unit built in. However, outside units beyond reverb are sometimes desirable to modify the sound.

For application of effect boxes, refer to the manufacturer's instructions or talk to someone who is well-versed in the particular unit. One note: effects tend to decrease the highs acoustically; musically, they can give the illusion of increasing the highs of the harmonics by brightening the sound and removing irritation. They can also cause problems. Lots of things can cause problems. A gig without some kind of sound reinforcement problem is a gig to be treasured.

Sound Reinforcement Problems and Solutions

▶ *Your system emits a loud hum.* This is a grounding problem. Check the grounds on the mixing board and on the stage. They should be earth grounded. An earth ground is anything that goes into the earth, such as a water pipe or a support pipe. You may have to change power sources.

▶ *Your system emits a loud buzz.* Boy, is this common. This is a bleed-through electrical problem. Check all the audio lines to see that none crosses an electrical line. Check the main power source to see if the lighting runs off the same source; if so, change to another power setup. If you still have a buzz, check to see if the club uses dimmer switches. If it does, you'll need an isolation transformer to get rid of the buzz. If this is a one-night showcase, live with the buzz.

▶ *Your system emits no sound at all, not even air noise.* Check all audio hookups from the mike to the snake to the board. Check the power and special connections. Make sure the amps and mixing board are plugged in. Make sure all mike/line switches are on "mike." Check the attenuation controls to be sure they are all turned up past the one-third mark.

▶ *Your system emits air noise, but no audio sound.* Check the entire system—you have a break in the line.

▶ *Your system emits loud variable sounds that go in and out.* The effects have been hooked up wrong. Isolate the unit to the instrument or mike it's supposed to be affecting and rewire.

▶ *Your system emits a booming noise.* This is probably a midrange adjustment mistake. Midranges have feedback points that are different for every room. The general rule for midrange adjustments is to increase all midranges until you hit the feedback loop and back off from there.

Feedback is defined as the reamplification of the existing signal, and a feedback loop is the beginning point of feedback. General rules for feedback include the following:

1. Don't run the mike gains too high.

2. Don't point mikes at the speakers or stand in front of a speaker with a mike.

3. Drop the main volume control immediately at feedback and bring it back up slowly. Check each mike to find the source of feedback and correct the positioning or EQ, as appropriate. Back off the gain of the mike until the loop is gone.

▶ *You are missing the top end of a musical source, such as a guitar.* This is called "clipping" and occurs because the amp doesn't have enough power or the speaker power demands aren't being met. (The power requirements are stated on the back of the speaker.) You have to add power or reduce the speaker needs by adding another amp or getting more efficient speakers. For example, if a speaker is rated 100 watts maximum RMS (Roots Means Squared), it needs two-and-a-half times as much power to efficiently drive it, or 250 watts of power. Power does not translate into loudness; power translates into clarity. If you have to perform now and there is no time for equipment changes or balancing, the rule of thumb is: volume aside, if all components including the voices cannot be heard with clarity, then the EQing is inaccurate and needs to be reviewed.

▶ *Your speakers crackle and buzz.* Too much power is going through the speakers. What you're hearing is voice coils burning up inside your speaker. This isn't good. Add speakers or cut the power back.

▶ *Instruments are too loud onstage* and the vocals are suffering for it. Bring the instruments down, rather than take the voices up. Check the house along with the monitors. If the problem is occurring only onstage, adjust the monitors. If the voices are also weak in the audience, adjust instruments across the board—speakers and monitors.

LIGHTING

The purpose of stage lighting is to create a feeling or mood that can't be created any other way. The important aspects of stage lighting are color, placement, movement, and feeling. To begin with, though, you need to be aware of the different types of lighting that are available to you.

Spotlights are the lights most people know about. They are run from the back of the room or hall and are high-power lights directed on one performer at a time, or at a close-standing duet. They are used to accent a specific performance. They can be used as white light or colored with lenses for more effects.

A *beam projector,* also run from the back of the room, covers a large area with light but has no focus and cannot be used with a lens. It is for lighting up a large portion of the stage, rather than narrowing in on the star or front.

Floodlights are reflector-type lights. They use high power to flood the entire stage with light, with no focus. They use colored glass rather than changeable lenses.

Strip lights are a fixed row of bare light bulbs that can be used with or without color.

Footlights are located at the foot or the sides of the stage and are recessed into the floor. They are bulbs with covers and gel slips, which provide varied color and life to the stage area.

An *arc light* is primarily used to light the backdrops on the stage.

Ellipsoidal spots are one of the most common light sources. They are built into rigs about the stage, in groups of up to forty or fifty lights. They can highlight changing areas of the stage as the show progresses.

Par lights are single element lights with gel racks and colored gels on each light. They are the most-used lights in the clubs. Whether the stage is large or small, par lights will be used above and forward of the stage to accent each player.

Color. Primary colors in lighting are red, blue, and green. Violet, orange, and indigo are secondary colors. The idea is to mix these colors to highlight, accent, modify, or brighten different elements of your show. Footlight colors and onstage colors are usually red and blue with white for highlighting. Offstage spots are generally yellow or pink for accent purposes. They keep you from looking washed out or bland. Stage lights that are yellow or green often have the unfortunate effect of making you look sickly or even deathly; these colors should be used only from a distance.

Light Placement. There are six places to put lighting: above, below, in front, stage left, stage right, and behind, for backlighting. In most small clubs, all of your lighting is above. This is called rig or rack lighting. When a system is above the stage, it is "being flown." Some stages also have openings in them and can be lit for interesting different effects; hence, the lighting comes from below. Spotlights and footlights are considered to be in front of the stage, even though the footlights are actually built into the stage. The most commonly used kind of spotlight is called a "super trouper" spot; it has fifteen different colored gels and is used to follow a performer. Light trees, strip lights, or side footlights are placed stage left and stage right. These provide accenting and general stage color. Arc lights are essentially the only lights behind the stage. They are also used for backlighting.

Movement. The illusion of movement is created by changing the colors of the lights or by switching on lights that were off and vice versa. Don't change color patterns too rapidly, because that can tire and irritate your audience. Make a smooth transition between primary colors. You can also use a "follow" spot to create movement by following the front as he moves around, or by moving the spot from player to player as a way of focusing the audience's attention to where you want it. You need a good operator who can anticipate your movements and a lighting rehearsal so that he can have a script of when to move the light and to whom.

Feeling. Feelings, or changes of emotions, through lighting, are achieved by using the warm colors (red, yellow, pink, indigo, orange) in contrast with the cool colors (blue, green, violet) in a changing flow. You need a controlled change of color, placement, and brightness onstage at all times to convey the mood or idea of the song that is being performed. Again, this requires a lighting rehearsal and a specifically scripted show to coordinate correctly.

The Light Board. All of the lights should be controlled through one light board, which is operated by the lighting technician. There are three kinds of light boards: fully manual, preset, and fully automatic. The light board controls are called "variable resisters" (VRs) and dimmers. Each VR controls the electricity used by each light, by varying the voltage. One VR can control a group of lights or "bundle." Most light boards will have the VRs arranged in groups of six with two rows, or twelve VRs, on the top and two rows on the bottom. These will refer back to a series of lights and a specific color in the series, per VR. For example, a row of six VRs may control the footlights onstage; the first VR controls all of the red footlights, the second VR controls all of the blue footlights, and so on.

On a manual light board, the VRs are moved up and down by hand. "Up" means all the power to the light is "on," or the light is bright; "down" means the least power is "on," or the light is dim.

On a preset board, you can fade between two settings by setting the upper board to one color scheme and the bottom board to another. When the top colors fade out, the bottom colors fade in. This is known as a "break scene change."

A fully automatic board has a computer for a brain. When you do your lighting rehearsal, you can manually set up all of the changes that will be necessary during the show and feed them into the brain's memory. The computer numbers all of the VR changes, so that you can call up a single change or replay the entire show. Depending on the system you have, the brain will be able to catalog as many as one thousand separate commands or lighting cues. Most fully automatic boards use cassettes or floppy disc storage units. After making a tape or disc, you will have a permanent record of that light show for that script, which you can use on any compatible board.

PROPS AND STAGE EFFECTS

Props and stage effects are devices that you can use to create or develop your group's image, stage performance, or trademark. They are not essential when working in local clubs, but they can be very effective in making your band out-of-the-ordinary and memorable. For showcasing or concert work they are almost mandatory, since most audiences, conditioned to visual stimuli by television, have come to expect larger-than-life audiovisual entertainment. The exception to this rule would be the solo ballad singer of the black-tie or long-gown genre, in which a show presentation is strictly one person out front, orchestra behind.

There are three kinds of props: hand-held, such as chains, snakes, dead chickens, and hats; set props, including chairs, rugs, cloth coverings, and boxes or stools to sit or stand on; and dress props which decorate the stage, and include curtains, pictures, banners, wall hangings, and large movie or video screens.

Stage effects are essentially concert devices. Laser shows, smoke or fog screens, flashpots, and fire or explosions all involve an element of danger and should never be used in a small room, or without a trained operator to control them. Don't underestimate the safety measures necessary to pull off these effects. Even something as simple as a smoke screen or fog device can cause physical injury to the person operating it or to the entire band—not to mention the audience—if it's not the right kind of device, not used with adequate ventilation, or controlled by someone who is busy performing onstage. In the clubs and in the small showcase rooms it's best to stick to props that are easily controlled.

4

TAPES AND VIDEOS

Audiotapes and videotapes will not become obsolete in the near future. New technology does not generally replace older forms of music presentation. If it did, radio, live theater, 45s, and long-playing records would no longer be with us. The latest discoveries usually serve to modify, advance, and supplement the standard forms. A&R men still listen to endless numbers of cassette tapes looking for a new group or hit single for their record companies. These days they also audition groups in action by reviewing videotaped performances. You can use this technology to promote your group to A&R men and other industry insiders. You can also use it to get more club work or to launch a career as a soloist. Tapes and videos are here to stay, and if you are to compete in the music industry, you'll have to know how to plan them, produce them, and get them into the hands of the right people.

Demo Tapes

IN TODAY'S music world, "We'll put a tape together!" has replaced the cry "Let's put on a show!" Everyone wants to record their music so they can send it to club owners, agents, record company executives, publishing houses, and songwriting contests. A demo tape is probably the best way to present yourself, your band, or your material to people who can give you work or further your career.

DETERMINING THE NEED

First, you must decide what you are trying to accomplish with your audiotape. Are you demoing your original tunes so that they can be sold to established artists? Or are you making a cover tune tape to show off what the band sounds like? Or are you trying to demonstrate your own solo abilities?

If you are trying to sell your original tunes to established artists, or if you are promoting yourself as a solo singer or instrumentalist (with or without a backup group), then you want to make a relatively simple recording illustrating just the specific thing you want to sell, whether it be the song, your voice, or your instrumental ability.

If you are trying to promote your band by doing original music or by demoing a few cover tunes, then you will want to produce the tape with the idea of the full recording or live performance in mind. On a demo of cover tunes, for example, use all the instrumentation and production that you would normally use on a stage. On a demo of originals use the instrumentation and production that you'd like to put on an airplay recording. Remember, though, that if you put in every single layer, every single harmony, every single bit of production that is possible on an originals demo, there will be nothing left for a producer to do—if one decides to pick you up. Egos are involved here, and nobody is going to want to work with you without having something to say about the product he's working on. So go ahead and produce the demo, but don't stuff or overproduce it. Leave a little room for a producer to add, subtract, or rearrange, as he sees necessary.

PICKING THE STUDIO AND ENGINEER

Once you know what you are trying to record, it is easier to find the right studio and engineer. Unless you are actually recording an album, you really don't need to spend money on a forty-eight- or fifty-six-track studio. Eight, sixteen, or twenty-four tracks should be enough to give you clarity of all the elements you wish to put into your demo. Make sure that the studio you pick has a separate control room apart from the main recording room. Make sure it has a separate headphone system per channel so that everyone can get all or part of the mix. If you are using a piano on your tape, find a studio that has one already tuned to the room. All of the equipment in the studio should be in good working condition, regardless of excuses, including at least two kinds of vocal effect units (such as digital delay, echo, and reverb). Most important, listen to some of the tapes that the studio or engineer has already produced. Do you like the sound? Your stuff will sound like that, because engineers record the way they hear, not the way you want them to hear. The engineer goes with the studio in most cases, especially in eight-to-sixteen-track studios, so if you don't like the way previous groups have come out of a particular studio, it probably isn't where you want to record.

PICKING THE MUSIC

Four-song demos are a standard in the industry, whether originals or cover tunes. Pick four tunes that fit into the same basic format. Don't try to impress someone with your versatility on a tape. Put your strongest song first, next strongest second, and so on. Cover tune tapes do not have to include ballads; it is assumed that every band can play a few ballads. Try to make sure that all four tunes follow the same groove but sound different. In other words, they should all fall within the same general category (such as top 40), yet the "feel" and rhythms should be varied enough that you don't sound boring halfway through the second song. If you're recording an originals tape and all of your music does sound essentially the same, vary the feel of the songs by using different production techniques for each tune. For example, if you write easy listening MOR songs that all have the same rhythm and flow, use strings to sweeten one tune, woodwinds for another, and so forth. The point is to keep the interest level as high as possible for the listener.

If this is a tape to demonstrate just the songs and you are doing a simple instrumental and voice demo, make sure that your melody lines are different enough not to be redundant. The use of different light production touches will help to break up any similarity between songs.

PREPRODUCTION

It is important to have a script before going into the studio to spend your money. What you're scripting are songs. This is called "preproduction." You must preproduce your tunes as fully as possible before ever stepping into that black hole of disappearing dollars. Studio time gets eaten up faster than you think it does. No engineer in his right mind is going to hurry you along when you're paying thirty dollars or sixty-five dollars or even a hundred and twenty dollars an hour for him to wait while you discuss whether the guitar player should do a solo all the way through the head or just through the bridge. A studio man who tells you to just relax and rehearse it up a little before you get started rolling tape, who encourages you to take your time and not worry about his schedule, is probably sitting back and thinking about the new VCR he's going to buy with the money you're wasting while you do just that. Be smart; preproduce.

Preproduction translates into nonstudio rehearsal time and discussion of exactly what parts are going to be laid down on each tune, instrument by instrument. You'll have to plan where all the solos are going and where all the harmonies are going on the recording. Keep in mind that a recorded performance is not the same as a live performance, so you may want to use different sounds, solos, and backup voices than you do when you play in a club. Have all solos, harmonies, leads, backups, drum breaks, string lines, horn fills, and special musical effects planned and rehearsed before walking through the door of the endless dollar. Know the exact order in which the four songs are going to be laid down—no last minute, "I really think the other song should go first" type of in-fighting should be done on the clock.

LAYING IT DOWN

When you go to the studio, take one or two reels of quarter-inch tape with you. Know in advance if you need to bring the half-inch, one-inch, or two-inch tape. For that matter, find out if your studio will permit you to bring in outside tape. They will definitely allow you to bring in quarter-inch tape; that is what your final mixdown will probably be on.

Bring any charts or sheet music that you need or that the studio musicians may need, if you've hired outside players or singers. These outside musicians will need specific charts with all the preproduction that you've worked out. Without charts, you will spend a lot of time describing what you want and where you want it. That time will cost you studio money and money for the musicians.

Bring to the studio all of the instruments that you'll need that the studio doesn't supply. You might also want to bring any instrument that you're particularly comfortable using, whether the studio has another one there or not. If possible, bring a producer or representative to act as a go-between for you and the engineer. If you have your own engineer and want him to do the session, be aware that the house engineer will not relinquish complete control of his equipment, in all probability, nor should he; after all, he is most familiar with the peculiarities of his equipment. Your engineer may be able to assist or co-engineer. However, this kind of arrangement should be worked out ahead of time with the house engineer (not with the receptionist or the marketing rep) so that valuable studio time is not spent working out everyone's function. It's also a good idea to make sure that the house engineer doesn't get irritated and decide not to give that extra amount of effort that could make your recording something special. Using tact and remaining aware of egos and politics is often more effective than bluntly being right.

Plan on spending between one and two hours setting up and getting levels and sounds nailed down. At least some of this time should be given to you gratis. You should have your setup time down pat; getting levels and sounds nailed down, on the other hand, can take an exasperatingly long time. If you aren't prepared for the annoying seventy-minute drum-miking delay, you could easily blow your cool and be completely worthless by the time you start rolling tape.

When the tape is ready to roll, lay down all the basic tracks for all the tunes, one after the other. You may have to repeat tracks or sections of tunes several times to get down exactly what you want. Since you're taking the time and money to go into a studio, you really should lay it down the best way you can.

After recording the basic tracks—drums, bass, piano, rhythm guitar—lay down the "sweetening": horn lines, strings, percussion, or whatever else the tune may require. Use "scratch" or practice vocals to work against, if necessary. Scratch vocals are recorded on a separate track at the same time as the basic track recording, then erased later. After all of the instruments are on tape, do the lead vocals, harmonies, and backups in that order or concurrently. If this is a simple instrument and vocal recording you can use either a scratch vocal or simply perform the tune live all the way through, then go back to fix whatever sections might need redoing.

MIXDOWN

When the recording is complete, the most important phase begins: the mixdown. The mixdown shapes the music and can be the saving grace of your tape—or the kiss of death.

It is generally recommended that you don't mix down on the same day that you do the recording. If you mix down on another day you will have a fresh perspective. If that isn't possible, at least take a break so that your head has a chance to clear and your ears have a chance to retune.

Pay close attention to what is happening during the mixdown and don't rely on the engineer to do it his way. At this point, you can bring the vocals up front or back off the harmonies; you can pull the guitar forward for its solo and tone it down for the head; you can essentially rearrange the vitality of the tune by the way you position the eight, sixteen, or twenty-four tracks in relation to each other.

When the mix is finished on the first tune, it should be transferred to the two-track (quarter-inch) master. Listen to this two-track very carefully on small five-inch or six-inch speakers rather than on the studio control-room monitors. Large, fine speakers will give you a false sense of your recording, especially when you remember that your tape is going to be listened to by people using home stereo equipment, portable cassette players or, most likely of all, automobile tape players. Mix down each tune separately and transfer it to the two-track master before going on to the next tune.

Your two-track tape is now a first generation tape, from which you can make a second generation cassette. If your studio is well-equipped, you can possibly make a first generation cassette at the same time that you're making the two-track master. If possible, always make copies from the first generation tape or cassette, as each additional generation forfeits a perceptible degree of clarity. High speed duplications should be checked before leaving the studio or duplication store to be sure that the recording came out complete and clear.

Audio Preproduction Checklist

1. Decide on the number of songs to be recorded.

2. Choose or compose the songs and prepare the arrangements.

3. Determine the duration of each song.

4. Prepare a basic instrumental breakdown, per song,
   per recording session.

5. Prepare a breakdown of lead and backup vocals.

6. Figure the total number of tracks you'll need (4, 8, 16, or more).

7. Schedule the musicians.

8. Program electronic instruments.

9. Prepare a timetable of the number of studio hours needed for:
   Basic tracks
   • instrument setup (usually on free time)
   • microphone placement
   • direct line setup
   • recording
   Overdubs (sweetening)
   Mixdown

10. Determine cost in dollars or percentage.

Videos

LIKE AUDIOTAPES, videos can be used to illustrate both original music and cover tunes. Unlike audiotapes, however, videos provide a wide variety of ways to make your musical statement.

DETERMINING THE NEED

Videos can be used for employment purposes or for airplay. A video for employment is essentially a recording of a live or studio performance to illustrate to a buyer what you sound and look like onstage, and how you'll be performing in his club or hall. Airplay videos are used to promote the band overall or to showcase and promote a specific song. Sometimes it is possible for the two needs to overlap. Generally, however, a video made for employment will not be airplay-worthy, and an airplay performance probably will not show off the band at enough length to cinch a gig.

PICKING THE CONCEPT

There are as many ways of shooting a video as your imagination can devise, so the first thing you should do after you identify the purpose for the video is to decide what kind of a format you're going to use.

There are three basic formats. The first is a live performance shoot, where the camera or cameras record you on location on stage as you would be seen by an audience. The second format is a studio performance, where either a straight concert situation similar to the first format is recorded, or a series of scenes are scripted and choreographed for the cameras. The third is drawn animation, computer animation, or a multiple image format where colors, shapes, or figures are drawn or photographed to create a mood, and no live footage is shot.

Many airplay videos now use combinations of all these formats. A combination, for example, of live, on-location shooting and in-studio footage (called a flip-flop) can be used for a story concept, where the lyrics of the tune are acted out through a series of scripted scenes. Using different formats may lead you to a variety of different concepts that you can use to sell your product. You can tell a story, you can have a visual display of emotion without a specific reference to the lyrics, or you can present a concert to your invisible audience.

For financial and practical reasons, most employment videos will be of the concert concept in either a live performance or a studio reproduction of a live performance. Airplay videos, on the other hand, can be whatever you want them to be, depending on what you are trying to sell and to whom.

If you are trying to sell your band to the public at large, such as on a local cable TV show, you might want to use the straight concert concept staged in a studio. This is certainly a workable format if the show is allowing you time for more than one song. On the other hand, you might want to use one of the other concepts that show off the band members with more varied camera work while still retaining the illusion of the song being sung. Such an approach might involve a story concept, using a mixture of in-studio and on-location scenes, with the band members lip syncing or pretending to play their instruments against a pre-recorded studio tape. This would be beneficial on a show where time for only one song is allotted and you want to make a deep impression quickly.

An important point to remember is that if your video is going to get you a gig, it will have to illustrate your performance on at least four tunes, just like an audiotape, so that the buyer has a chance to see you in action in lieu of an audition. That doesn't mean he'll watch the entire show, of course, but he'll want the full presentation to skim through. Airplay videos, on the other hand, are one song long unless you're doing an entire concert. (A concert on TV can be anywhere from twenty minutes to two hours long.)

Specialty concepts that go beyond one song will tax the audience's ability to follow and enjoy your presentation. You'll notice that TV video shows seldom present two of the same group's videos back-to-back without at least part of an interview in between.

After you've decided on the purpose of the video, the format you want and can afford, and the basic concept you want to use, you can start looking for a studio or director to shoot it.

PICKING THE STUDIO AND DIRECTOR

Video productions require video equipment, cameramen, audio equipment, an engineer, a director, and possibly an in-house studio. The right cameraman or director (they are sometimes one and the same) can make a world of difference to your finished product. If you're shooting with more than one camera, a good director is essential for picking and mixing the best shots from each camera into a smooth, flowing presentation. Make sure that the studio you pick is one you can afford without neurotically watching the clock. Make sure that all of the equipment is up-to-date and in good working condition. Make sure that the studio is equipped to do the kind of format and concept you have decided on using. If you're doing a live, on-location concert shoot, for example, be sure you pick people who are familiar with that kind of remote production. To check out a studio, call them and make an appointment. Any reputable studio will allow you to come in, look around, ask questions, and take a look at their work.

After you've found the people or house studio that fits all of your criteria, review some of the videos they've produced. Find out who the cameramen and director were on those you like. These are the people you'll want to work with, even if they're not part of the regular staff. If you're told that the staff people are "just as good," review some of their tapes. If they're not "just as good" or, more specifically, just what you want, keep looking. A good production staff or director should be able to help you develop your own sketchy ideas of what you want to present into an actual screen display that satisfies your intent. The wrong director or a production-line outfit will give you what he or they are most familiar with or find easiest to do, rather than what you are trying to express. You will probably need a director to preproduce your video; however, you should start with a firm idea of what you want to say.

PICKING THE MUSIC

This will not be a major problem if you're creating a single-tune airplay video, since you'll obviously use the tune that you're trying to sell. If this is a half-hour TV concert or an employment presentation, however, the music that you pick can be crucial. Use the tunes that best represent the band's recognized musical groove and lend themselves well to a visual presentation. Because they do need to be visually impressive, they may not necessarily be your four strongest tunes, musically. Try to pick songs with extreme tempos, that is, either slow ballads that can be enhanced with lighting to create an intimate mood, or dynamic, fast-paced tunes that are good for showcasing onstage antics and personalities. Try to avoid medium-tempo and long-running songs, where little can be done visually to break up the song. This kind of tune can easily translate into visual boredom.

LAYING IT DOWN

As with an audiotape or, for that matter, any professional performance, script the presentation before you get to the studio. Do as much preproduction as you can. Meet with the director ahead of time to nail down the specifics before you go in to do the shoot. Try to work out what you're going to lay down scene by scene; this is called "storyboarding." Storyboarding includes knowing the song or order of the songs, knowing the stage moves and any applicable choreography, and knowing what scenes will be called for and where and how they're going to be shot.

If you are doing a concert concept, play to the camera as if it were a member of the audience. Look toward the camera and sometimes at it, but don't rivet your eyes on the lens and don't totally ignore it. With video productions, the fate of the final product is essentially in the hands of the director and cameraman. Therefore, make sure you've done your homework up front and you and the director or cameraman have hammered out all the finer points before the tape rolls. Then make sure you follow the directions you're given. And don't forget to relax.

Using Your Finished Product

TAPES AND videos can be used for two basic purposes: to gain immediate employment or to promote your long-range career plans. If you've made a tape or video of cover tunes or originals for employment reasons, plan on it being a short-term sales tool. Employment devices should be done as simply and economically as possible, since they will be reviewed briefly and will quickly become obsolete. Present your product to as many agents, managers, and owners as you can in order to secure a gig and figure that if the gig runs for a long time, you'll need a new tape or video when you go for a new job.

If your finished product is meant to promote industry attention or bring financial returns, you have a number of choices about what to do with it. Most musicians, after reading all the trade magazines and absorbing all the television and radio pap, will either send their product through the mail to an A&R man or decide to do an independent label or a vanity press release. This is a good way to run along with the pack, and there is no guarantee that it won't work for you. There is an excellent chance, however, that you're merely giving away your money. To be most effective and to actually have a shot at being heard by the right person or people, you have to start with some careful planning and research.

SELLING THE SONG

First, recall the reason you made the tape or video. Are you trying to sell the performance or are you trying to sell the music? If you're trying to sell the music, you've made a reasonably simple audiotape that can be presented to publishers, A&R men, or individual artists.

Most publishers and A&R men will tell you that the tape isn't produced enough for them to be able to know what the record will sound like. Therefore, what you really want to do is get your song to the artist you want to sell it to.

Make a list of the established artists you think might be interested in the kind of song or songs you've recorded. Do whatever research is necessary to find out who their personal managers are and how to reach them. Then focus your efforts on getting your tape heard by those managers who are aware of their artists' needs and wants, and who can get your tunes placed on an album, if they're liked. You should be aware, however, that the industry systems are set up to prevent just this kind of personal contact. You will invariably be told to contact agents, publishers, and record companies—in short, to follow standard operating procedures. Following those standard procedures could eventually lead you to the sale of your tunes. Hundreds of songs do filter up through the millions of tunes submitted each year, and do get bought and recorded. However, if you've put all your best efforts into your product just to send it through the industry production line, plan on spending a lot of time waiting around to find out you've been rejected.

If you have no specific artist in mind for your tunes, the best course to take is to research the needs of the various record companies and publishers. Find out exactly who is looking for your type of material at this time (not what they've got out now—that's old news) and how to get it to the person who makes the decisions about unsolicited material. If possible, present your tape in person and meet the individual so that yours is not just another faceless, nameless product.

Some of the different kinds of companies you can research are: local labels, independent labels, national and international labels, foreign labels, and corresponding publishers in all those areas. Be sure that you've checked with a lawyer or accountant ahead of time so that you have some idea of what you can expect to sell your product for and what the current new-songwriter deals are looking like. This is true even if you have hired an agent or manager to do the peddling for you. Never relinquish control of what is happening to your musical product, or depend on an intermediary to automatically make the best deal for you.

SELLING THE GROUP

If you have made a tape or video with the idea of selling the performers and the performance of the material, you have a less clear-cut course. Trade magazines are filled with managers, production companies, cable TV stations, publishers, and independent labels or producers looking for new artists and material. You'll note that they are never the big-name, nationally known companies. Start by mapping out a specific campaign that you feel you can afford to follow, with a specific goal to aim for. For example, you might want this video or tape to be reviewed eventually by CBS records. You may simply want to be sure that you sell out your complete stock of vanity press albums. Write down the goal and combine your recorded exposure efforts with your live performance efforts to achieve the goal as quickly as possible. Try to avoid setting nebulous or hard-to-reach goals. Aim for getting your video reviewed by the right person; work backward from that goal to finding out who that person is and how to get in touch with him.

Since your tape or video is essentially another tool to be used in your drive for advancement in the music industry, remember that there are literally dozens of ways you can exploit its marketing potential. Refer back to your five-year plan to see how your finished recorded product can be used to push you from where you are to the next level you hope to attain.

When you're selling a band or an individual artist and you have a taped presentation of the performance, an enthusiastic agent or manager can become extremely valuable. They are not mandatory, though. On your own initiative you can submit your material to independent production companies; local and cable television stations; local, college, and major radio stations; local record stores; club owners; concert promoters; independent, local, national, and foreign record labels; specific production firms who book major television or concert and club productions; the public at large, through sales from the stage, sales through public advertising, or sales to your personal following by mail. Nevertheless, you will find that many companies, especially those that are most sought-after, refuse to review unsolicited material. For these efforts, you will need an agent or manager. Pick one with care. Make sure he's reliable, enthusiastic about you, and financially solvent. But make sure that you've mapped out a specific campaign, and aren't just relying on your intermediary to take care of everything.

Whether you are marketing your product independently or through an agent or other intermediary, make sure you are taking full advantage of every opportunity you can create to use your recording as a sales tool. Don't let the life of the product fade away through the passing of time, which can have a damaging effect on your recorded efforts. Even the best performance on tape will start to feel stale and old to you after a while, despite the fact that it is still new to the public and the industry. After you've recorded, get out and sell.

5

THE NEXT STEP

After you've mastered your axe, put your band together, booked the gig, advertised the show, and recorded the demo, you're ready to embark on the next stage of your career. You've got a lot of decisions to make before you get started, and an endless number of factors to consider once you get rolling. Among them are the issues of advancing technology, playing on the road, and signing contracts. In the final analysis, however, it is your attitude and your energy that will make or break your career. Can you make it? Keep on pushing forward and find out for yourself.

Technological Advances

THE ARRIVAL and acceptance of MIDI (Musical Instrument Digital Interface) and other new electronic devices have altered the face of contemporary music.

For many musicians, so-called "canned music" is grounds for taking up arms. On one side there are the technically oriented players and producers who see the new electronics as an exciting tool that increases efficiency, opens up possibilities for new sounds, and reduces musical headaches. Got a drummer who's never on time? Use a drum machine. Want a sound that is physically impossible for a human to create? Use a digital sampler. There is some piece of equipment to replace every instrumental sound possible or conceivable, along with a fair number of vocal sounds. On the other side, however, you have highly trained, emotional players who believe that the essence of music comes from the soul of the musician, not just from the notes that he plays, and that the new technology represents a threat to individual players. The battle goes on.

If you, as an individual artist or part of a group, are trying to reach a median ground in all of this and foresee what kind of future lies ahead for the live performer, keep in mind that people don't shower, dress, and leave the house to watch machines. People still like to see people, and it doesn't look like this universal preference is about to undergo any radical change in the near future. It is therefore up to you to use the devices that are available to augment your sound and enhance your performance, but don't be afraid that they will actually replace you over the long haul. Remember, it takes people to operate, program, and express themselves on electronic equipment. And as for the equipment itself, the novelty of new technology for its own sake will wear off as time goes on. People become jaded very easily in this day and age. Already they are beginning to rediscover simpler, less esoteric sounds. Eventually alien, unrecognizable synthesizer sounds will become a novelty again, rather than the norm. Also bear in mind that fantastic studio creations using real sound samples do not translate well to live performance without enough people on stage playing instruments so that audience members can feel comfortable and familiar with what they are watching.

To respond to the pressure on you, the live performer, from these new marvels, use the current trends as an excuse to learn that vital second instrument (especially if you do not already play keys) or expand your vocal abilities, thereby making yourself that much more viable and irreplaceable.

The Union

THE AMERICAN Federation of Musicians exists in almost every city and town in the United States. As with all labor organizations, the A.F. of M. has established guidelines for working hours and conditions and for minimum pay scales. It offers a pension plan and health insurance to its membership. As your career advances and you begin to play for more money, you will undoubtedly have to join the union, since it regulates most of the higher paying, more established gigs. When you're starting out, however, most of your gigs will probably be at smaller, non-union venues. Since the union sets minimum pay standards, it would be worth your while to know what that scale is, so you'll have some idea of whether you're being underpaid on a gig. The union also stipulates that a musician and his employer must have a written contract. This is a good rule to follow whether or not you are a union member. A standard engagement contract will identify the employer and the band, the starting and finishing dates of the gig, the days and hours of the performance, and the amount and terms of payment. Additional items may be added depending on the special requirements of the employer or the particular needs of the band.

Be assured that eventually you will come in contact with the musicians' union, so it is a good idea to begin familiarizing yourself with their regulations and rules for membership. To find out this information, contact the local office of the A.F. of M. in your area.

Roadwork

FOR THE nonsigned, not-a-major-act musician, there are two ways to exist on the road: making money and losing money. And always the twain shall meet.

At some time or other every musician gets a hankering to "go on the road," either to steady down the act, see the world, or just make some good money. Road gigs, as a general rule, do pay more than in-town gigs. Road gigs, as another general rule, cost a great deal more than in-town gigs. How can that be when you've signed with a good agency who is going to get you rooms with every gig, keep you in a tight traveling area, and make sure you work constantly? You don't have to pay rent, right? Almost right.

Take a close look at your road contract. Chances are it will guarantee forty weeks of work out of every fifty-two. That leaves twelve weeks every year that you are not guaranteed work. Expect to be off those twelve weeks. Now, if you got that time all at once, you could come to ground, find a local job, and play a neighborhood bar for three months, never losing any money. Down time, however, doesn't come in clumps; down time comes in one- and two-week increments, during which you are nowhere near home or family. You'll have to find a place to stay, a way to eat, and something to do with your time.

When you go on the road and are planning expenses, always take into account the cost of having time on your hands. The cost of being on the road includes lodging (for those times when rooms somehow don't materialize), food, equipment emergencies, travel, vehicle maintenance expenses and, most costly, boredom money. Boredom money is spent on video games, pizza, beer, movies, and shopping for miscellaneous things you don't need but feel like buying. Musicians who have a lot of time to kill and who become understandably paranoid about equipment failure are often seen haunting local music stores and paying outrageous prices for duplicate and triplicate gear.

So, who can realistically expect to make money on the road? People who have good contingency plans, and who know how to go into a strange town and immediately find a reputable doctor or mechanic; people who travel with such alternate lodging as a trailer or tent setup; people who can service their own vehicles and equipment; married couples who can cut the cost of down time and pool their paychecks; singles, who have low equipment needs and can make use of commercial transportation.

Of course, the time will come (hopefully) when your group goes on a concert tour. The difference in being on the road this way is that you are embarking on a self- or privately financed promotional tour and it is to someone's advantage that you fulfill all your contracted gigs. Don't get cocky, though; you're nothing but fresh meat once you're outside your own backyard, no matter how big that backyard may be.

A few cautionary words are indicated for the band that is just embarking on its first concert tour: don't rely on college radio, the mails, or phone calls to verify your tour gigs. Send a personal representative to shake hands on all impending deals; you'll find the results to be invaluable. Advance men can mean the difference between a successful tour and a truly botched fiasco. Also, don't screw around with high-profile groups who have massive economic power or backing. You'll end up the loser if you put yourself in the position of being an irritant to established money.

Contracts

THE MORE your career picks up steam, the more you'll be dealing with various types of contracts. Common ones include partnership agreements between band members, which usually provide guidelines for dividing responsibilities, sharing profits and losses, and terminating the partnership; agreements with agents and managers; contracts with publishers and record companies; and contracts for specific concert appearances or nightclub engagements.

Basically, contracts imply notice and specify money. At the club level, contracts are an advanced form of a handshake, and are only as good as the word of the person signing them. However, this is a fluid business; that person may not be there next week to honor what you signed. Any contract can be taken to court, but that doesn't mean it is necessarily enforceable. Furthermore, a judgment in your favor over a contract dispute doesn't guarantee monetary satisfaction.

Corporate contracts for chains or agencies are written strictly for the corporation; they usually guarantee you nothing that you can even take to court. Group contracts that bind you to various restrictions when you leave the group (such as not playing in the area for two years) may not be enforceable, but can cause incredible problems until that is proven. Don't get hooked into signing a contract that is really designed to exploit you rather than bind you to an equitable deal. In other words, the basic rule of thumb when approaching contracts is know what you're signing.

Research

THE CONCEPT of research cannot be emphasized enough. Research your personnel before hiring them. Research the group you're going to join, the club you want to play, the studio you want to record in, the buyers you want to approach, the name you want to protect, the avenues and expenses of advertising in your area, the needs of the labels and producers you want to impress, and the ways of gathering financial and physical support. Research anything you are asked to sign. Even if you have to spend a lot of money to get a decent legal opinion on what you're about to do, remember that you are protecting yourself from risking tenfold the price without the counsel. Know what you are doing as you move from one stage of the business to the next. The other guy will probably know what he's doing. Always remember that music is a self-employed business and, consequently, you and you alone will bear the brunt of your self-created mistakes. The key to having the odds on your side is knowing what you're getting into. Research.

Career Options

YOU CAN have a successful career in the music business, even if you never make it to the top, and even if you don't want to try to get there. The only people who are forced to drop out of the music business and find other careers are the people who irreparably burn out, the people who have unrealistic and inflexible goals, and the people who simply can't cut the life-style or the audience's needs. Besides the much publicized level of stardom or national recognition, there are also the levels of studio or concert support, local celebrity-hood, and long–term or steady work in the clubs. You, as an individual, can be

▶ part of a tightly knit group that only performs as a unit (not individually) and builds its reputation within a large but confined geographical area;

▶ part of a group that normally works together but also allows its members to free-lance for casuals or studio work;

▶ a free-lance leader, sideman, or hired player who works in whatever situation arises;

▶ a single performer who works the club circuit or finds a "home" and becomes a local celebrity;

▶ a "weekend warrior" who makes his living in another field but plays casuals and weekend club gigs.

These are all reasonable and viable possibilities.

If you have decided that you are going to be a musician for life, or if, as is so often the case, your personal needs have decided for you, then it is not essential for you to achieve international fame. It would be nice, but not attaining that rank doesn't mean your music isn't as important or as good as the music of those who have reached the top. Being successful in the music business means having your music appreciated by your audience, however big that audience is, and achieving whatever level of financial return you feel you need to get from your music.

Regardless of where you top out, by conscious decision or by circumstance, pursuing your musical career on a long-term basis requires accumulating the skills of the craft. You'll need musical agility, a professional attitude, political acumen, and career foresight.

What You Need to Win

FEW MUSICIANS get into the business without initially hoping and believing that they will be one of those who will make it to the top. Unfortunately, only a few of them will. It takes a great deal more than raw talent and a lot of heart to climb that ladder all the way. It also takes technique, money, commitment, tenacity, a support group, and lots of luck. You can develop, find, or create every one of these elements and still end up playing neighborhood clubs. However, just because you can't always beat the odds doesn't mean you can't get them in your favor.

TALENT

The word talent refers to raw ability, either instrumentally or vocally. It also refers to the raw ability (physical or mental) that can be developed and can grow to provide a solid foundation for your career. The raw ability to take command of a stage can go a long way toward covering other inadequacies. However, talent without the ability to develop it is really just a gift; having an undeveloped gift becomes painful when the almost-made-its are weeded out from the did-make-its. You'll have to use your talent and build on it.

TECHNIQUE

Technique is the sum total of skills used in the execution of your craft. This includes the development of your raw musical talent, your political savvy, your professional attitude and deportment, your stage and audience control, and your personal performance abilities. It all adds up to being able to effectively use the talents and abilities you were born with, or worked to acquire. A word of caution: standards have come up tremendously in the last twenty years. You have to be better today than you were even five years ago, and in five years you'll have to be better than you are now. Kids coming out of college today know more about the basics of their music than players who have been working for years; you can't get away with simple ear training anymore. In essence, the crowd you're going to run with is going to be a fast one, no matter how low a level you start at. Make sure you can memorize repertoire; make sure you stay abreast of current techniques, and musical trends. This is all part of developing and using that raw talent you have.

MONEY

How much money will you need? Enough to do the following:

▶ buy all the necessary equipment

▶ rent the rehearsal space

▶ pay for the demo tapes and videos

▶ advertise yourself and your gigs

▶ take pictures

▶ buy clothes

▶ develop a style and a show through lighting, sound, and effects

▶ pay for your support group

▶ pay for outside musical personnel when necessary

▶ pay for the packaging, phone calls, postage, and travel necessary to get your product (that is, you) to enough influential people that the odds of someone buying and promoting what you've got move in your favor.

And enough to pay the rent, buy the food—in other words, live—while all of this is going on. That's how much money you'll need, plus a little more for all the things you forgot and all the miscalculations you made. Plus a little more for emergencies and disasters.

COMMITMENT AND TENACITY

Tenacity is defined as the state of holding fast or firmly; being tough or obstinate. No matter what goes wrong, no matter how many times you're told "no," no matter what the odds are against you, or how many people oppose you, you still push on. You need a strong ability to accept and go beyond rejection, even if it's constant. You need a sustained passion for what you're doing and an unbreakable will to persevere. You also need the same commitment from your support group, both professional and personal.

YOUR SUPPORT GROUP

You need behind you a financial organization and an active support group that is dedicated to pushing your career upward. Bands and individual artists do not move their own careers; artists don't have credibility in the business world beyond a certain point. You want to have a support group that will go out on a limb for you, that will supply or help raise money, that is committed to your reaching your goals and that stands to get a return from your success, either personally, financially, or both.

LUCK

Luck is really opportunity. Opportunities are created by activity. Develop that five-year plan, even if you have to rewrite it a thousand times. Map out specific steps and put yourself on a timetable. Get yourself that support group and financial backing; push through the wall and beyond. Don't let a month, a week, even a day go by without some activity on your part to push ahead. The more effective activity you generate, the more opportunities you will breed. The more opportunities you breed, the more the law of averages swings in your direction—hence, "luck."

Never stop, and you won't be stopped.

Suggested Reading

Aebersold, Jamey, editor. *Jazz Play-A-Long Sets for All Instruments*. 41 vols. New Albany, Indiana (1211 Aebersold Drive, New Albany, IN 47150): Jamey Aebersold, c1987.

Bacon, Tony. *Rock Hardware*. New York: Harmony Books, 1981.

Baird, Jock, and others. "Understanding MIDI," special edition of *Musician,* Vol. I (1986), Vol. II (1987).

Billboard. New York: Billboard Publications, Inc. (Published weekly.)

Bronson, Fred. *The Billboard Book of Number One Hits*. New York: Billboard Publications, Inc., 1985.

Burton, Gary. *A Musician's Guide to the Road*. New York: Billboard Publications, Inc., 1981.

Csida, Joe. *The Music/Record Career Handbook*. Revised edition. New York: Billboard Publications, Inc., 1980.

Davis, Clive. *Clive: Inside the Record Business*. New York: William Morrow and Company, 1975.

Down Beat. Elmhurst, Illinois: Maher Publications. (Published monthly.)

Eargle, John. *The Microphone Handbook*. Plainview, New York: Elar Publishing Company, 1982.

Erickson, J. Gunnar, Edward R. Hearn, and Mark E. Holloran. *Musician's Guide to Copyright*. New York: Charles Scribner's Sons, 1983.

Frascogna, Xavier M., and H. Lee Heatherington. *Successful Artist Management*. New York: Billboard Publications, Inc., 1978.

Guitar Player. Cupertino, California: GPI Publications. (Published monthly.)

International Buyer's Guide. New York: Billboard Publications, Inc. (Published yearly.)

International Recording Equipment and Studio Directory. New York: Billboard Publications, Inc. (Published yearly.)

International Talent & Touring Directory. New York: Billboard Publications, Inc. (Published yearly.)

Keyboard. Cupertino, California: GPI Publications. (Published monthly.)

Martin, George, editor. *Making Music: The Guide to Writing, Performing, & Recording*. New York: Quill, 1983.

Mehegan, John. *Jazz Improvisation*. 4 vols. New York: Watson-Guptill Publications, 1962–1984. I, Tonal and Rhythmic Principles (1984). II, Jazz Rhythm and the Improvised Line (1962). III, Swing and Early Progressive Piano Styles (1964). IV, Contemporary Piano Styles (1965).

Miller, Jim, editor. *The Rolling Stone Illustrated History of Rock and Roll*. New York: The Rolling Stone Press, 1976.

Musician. Gloucester, Massachusetts: Amordian Press, Inc. (Published monthly.)

Pickow, Peter, and Amy Appleby. *The Billboard Book of Songwriting*. New York: Billboard Publications, Inc., 1988.

Rapaport, Diane S. *How to Make and Sell Your Own Records*. New York: Quick Fox Publishing, 1981.

Shemel, Sidney, and M. William Krasilovsky. *This Business of Music*. Fifth edition, revised and enlarged, including the latest copyright and tax information, updated forms, and an all new section on video rights. New York: Billboard Publications, Inc., 1987.

————. *More About This Business of Music*. Third edition, revised and enlarged. New York: Billboard Publications, Inc., 1982.

Stein, Howard, and Ronald Zalkind. *Promoting Rock Concerts: A Practical Guide*. New York: Schirmer Books, 1979.

Stokes, Geoffrey. *Star-Making Machinery: Inside the Business of Rock & Roll*. New York: Random House, 1977.

Whitburn, Joel. *The Billboard Book of Top 40 Albums*. New York: Billboard Publications, Inc., 1987.

————. *The Billboard Book of Top 40 Hits*. Third edition. New York: Billboard Publications, Inc., 1987.

Woram, John M. *The Recording Studio Handbook*. Plainview, New York: Elar Publishing Company, 1983.

Index

Senior Editor: Tad Lathrop
Art Director: Bob Fillie
Cover Design: Bob Fillie
Production Manager: Ellen Greene